C000278537

TRAVERSE
THEATRE

Traverse Theatre Company and the Barbican Centre (BITE:00)

Solemn Mass for

A Full Moon in Summer

by Michel Tremblay

translated by Martin Bowman and Bill Findlay

cast

Isabelle	Molly Innes
Yannick	John Kazek
Jeannine	Hope Ross
Louise	Elizabeth Millbank
Rose	Colette O'Neil
Mathieu	Liam Brennan
Gaston	David Gallacher
Mireille	Pauline Knowles
Yvon	Robert Carr
Gerard	Vincent Friell
The Widow	Ann Scott-Jones

directors	Philip Howard and Ros Steen
designer	Neil Warmington
lighting designer	Jon Linstrum
composer	Jon Beales
movement director	Struan Leslie
stage manager	Carrie Hutcheon
deputy stage manager	Victoria Paulo
assistant stage manager	Brendan Graham
wardrobe supervisor	Lynn Ferguson
wardrobe assistant	Caitlin Blair

**First performed at the Traverse Theatre
Friday 28 April; first performed at the Pit Theatre,
Barbican Centre, Wednesday 17 May 2000.**

Michel Tremblay

Born 1942 in Montreal, Michel Tremblay is Québec's most eminent playwright. He began writing plays, poems, short stories and novels while still at high school. The production of his first play *Les Belles-Soeurs* in 1968, is regarded as the single most significant event in the history of Québec theatre. Since then he has written a total of 24 plays, including *The House Among the Stars* (European Premiere at the Traverse Theatre, 1992), 3 musicals, 11 novels, numerous collections of short stories, 7 screenplays, an opera libretto and several translations and adaptations. His many awards and accolades include 4 doctorates.

Martin Bowman & Bill Findlay

are, respectively, a Canadian and a Scot. They have co-translated a number of other plays by Michel Tremblay: THE GUID SISTERS, THE REAL WURLD, HOSANNA, (Tron); THE HOUSE AMONG THE STARS (Traverse and Perth); FOREVER YOURS, MARIE-LOU (Ladderman); ALBERTINE IN FIVE TIMES (Clyde Unity). They also translated Québec playwright Jeanne-Mance Delisles's THE REEL OF THE HANGED MAN (Stellar Quines). Martin Bowman, with Majdi Mouawad, co-translated into French the stage adaptation of Irvine Welsh's TRAINSPOTTING (Théâtre de Quat'Sous, Montreal), and Enda Walsh's DISCO PIGS (Théâtre de Poche, Brussels). He teaches at Champlain College, St. Lambert, Québec, and is a Research Fellow in the Department of Drama, Queen Margaret University College, Edinburgh.

Bill Findlay adapted Gerhart Hauptmann's THE WEAVERS (Dundee Rep), Pavel Kohout's FIRE IN THE BASEMENT (Communicado), and Teresa Lubkiewicz's WEREWOLVES (Theatre Archipelago). He lectures in the Department of Drama, Queen Margaret University College, Edinburgh, and is editor of A HISTORY OF SCOTTISH THEATRE (1998).

BIOGRAPHIES

Jon Beales (composer): For the Traverse: THE SPECULATOR (co-production with Edinburgh International Festival), WORMWOOD. Other theatre work includes: THE GRAPES OF WRATH (7:84); KISSING ANGELS (National Youth Theatre); PETER PAN (Royal Lyceum); GREAT EXPECTATIONS (Pitlochry); THE SLEEPING BEAUTY (Dundee Rep); MARY QUEEN OF SCOTS GOT HER HEAD CHOPPED OFF (Byre); THE HOME-MADE CHILD and five further productions for Lung Ha's Theatre Co. As musical director: MOTHER COURAGE AND HER CHILDREN, HANSEL AND GRETEL (Royal Lyceum); WHISTLE DOWN THE WIND (Byre).

Liam Brennan (*Mathieu*): For the Traverse: QUARTZ, KING OF THE FIELDS, THE SPECULATOR (co-production with Edinburgh International Festival), FAMILY, KNIVES IN HENS (1997 Edinburgh Festival Fringe) and WORMWOOD. His other theatre work includes seasons and productions with Dundee Rep, Perth Rep, Royal Lyceum, Sheffield Crucible, Borderline, Cumbernauld Theatre, Salisbury Playhouse, Brunton Theatre, Byre Theatre, Durham Theatre Company and Calypso Productions, Dublin. Recent theatre performances include: Hamish in THINGS WE DO FOR LOVE (Royal Lyceum); Macbeth in MACBETH (Brunton); Edmund in KING LEAR and Michael Collins in GOD SAVE IRELAND CRIED THE HERO (Wiseguise). Liam's television appearances include roles in: TAGGART, STRATHBLAIR, HIGH ROAD and MACHAIR and also numerous plays and short stories for BBC Radio.

Robert Carr (*Yvon*): For the Traverse: KING OF THE FIELDS. Other recent theatre work includes STIFF! (Diva Productions), DEAD FUNNY, KIDNAPPED, CARLUCCO AND THE QUEEN OF HEARTS, MARY QUEEN OF SCOTS GOT HER HEAD CHOPPED OFF, TRAVESTIES, MIRANDOLINA, THE MARRIAGE OF FIGARO (Royal Lyceum), GONE FISHING, A SATIRE OF THE FOUR ESTAITES, NO EXPENSE SPARED (Wildcat), DUMBSTRUCK (Tron), THE BARBER OF SEVILLE (Arches). Film and TV includes Johnston, the Goat Farmer in MONARCH OF THE GLEN, Mr Leitch in ORPHANS, Haldene in THE CREATIVES, THE BALDY MAN, TAGGART, Harry MacLiesh in HAMISH MACBETH and Ferret in THE HIGH LIFE.

Vincent Friell (*Gerard*): Born and educated in Glasgow. For the Traverse: PERFECT DAYS (Traverse, Hampstead & tour, Vaudeville), TALLY'S BLOOD. Other theatre work includes: IN TIME OF STRIFE (7:84); THE LUCKY ONES, THE TEMPEST (TAG); SLAB BOYS TRILOGY, HARD TIMES, UNCLE VANYA, WHITE BIRD PASSES (Dundee Rep); THE PRIME OF MISS JEAN BRODIE (Brunton); MR GILLIE (Scottish Theatre Co.); DANTON'S DEATH (Communicado); AMERICAN BUFFALO (Winged Horse); WALTER (Edinburgh International Festival); THE HOUSE AMONG THE STARS (Perth Rep); THE SLAB BOYS TRILOGY (Young Vic); ARSENIC AND OLD LACE (Arches); NO EXPENSE SPARED (Wildcat); A WHOLLY HEALTHY GLASGOW (Dressing Room); SABINA! (Borderline); DON JUAN (Theatre Highland). Film includes: TRAINSPOTTING, RESTLESS NATIVES. Television work includes: TOUGHLOVE (Granada) TAGGART, WOMAN AT WAR, HIGH ROAD (STV); THE CREATIVES, END OF THE LINE, KNOCKBACK, RAB C NESBITT, PARAHANDY (BBC); COUNTRY DIARY OF AN EDWARDIAN LADY (Granada); ROUGHNECKS (First Choice).

David Gallacher *(Gaston):* David returns to Scottish theatre following a sabbatical of ten years, during which time he was a partner in an arboricultural practice, David's recent theatre work includes: DREAM TRAIN (Magnetic North) and FREE ROPE (Edinburgh International Festival for the Saltire Society). Recent film and television work includes: COMPLICITY, TAGGART and REBUS - BLACK AND BLUE.

Philip Howard (director): Trained at the Royal Court Theatre, London, on the Regional Theatre Young Director Scheme from 1988-90. He was Associate Director at the Traverse from 1993-96, and has been Artistic Director since 1996. Productions at the Traverse include LOOSE ENDS, BROTHERS OF THUNDER, EUROPE, KNIVES IN HENS (also Bush Theatre), THE ARCHITECT, FAITH HEALER, WORMWOOD, LAZYBED, THE CHIC NERDS, KILL THE OLD TORTURE THEIR YOUNG, HERITAGE, THE SPECULATOR (co-production with Edinburgh International Festival) and HIGHLAND SHORTS. Philip's other theatre includes HIPPOLYTUS (Arts Theatre, Cambridge), ENTERTAINING MR SLOANE (Royal, Northampton) and SOMETHING ABOUT US (Lyric Hammersmith Studio).

Molly Innes *(Isabelle):* For the Traverse: WIDOWS, SHINING SOULS, STONES AND ASHES, CROSS DRESSING IN THE DEPRESSION, DREAMING IN PUBLIC (Traverse & Byre). Other Theatre work includes:ELECTRA (Theatre Babel); TIMELESS (Suspect Culture), DOING BIRD (Cat A Theatre Co.); PLAYBOY OF THE WESTERN WORLD (Communicado); JEKYLL AND HYDE ,TO KILL A MOCKING BIRD, THE PRIME OF MISS JEAN BRODIE (Royal Lyceum); STINGING SEA (Citizens'); TARTUFFE (Dundee Rep); GLORIA GOODHEART AND THE GLITTER GRAB GANG, JOLLY ROBERT AND THE PIRATES FROM SPACE (Theatre Workshop); MURDER AND THE MUSIC HALL (Theatre Public). Film work includes: KARMIC MOTHERS (Tartan Short), RATCATCHER, STELLA DOES TRICKS. Television work includes: REBUS, LIFE SUPPORT, PSYCHOS, THE BILL, A MUGS GAME; TAKIN' OVER THE ASYLUM; THE FERGUSON THEORY; STRATHBLAIR; RAB C. NESBITT. Radio work includes: BILL 'N' KOO, SOME OF MY BEST FRIENDS ARE DOLPHINS, THE FOURTH FOREIGNER (BBC Radio Four).

John Kazek *(Yannick):* For the Traverse: KING OF THE FIELDS, PERFECT DAYS (Traverse, Hampstead & tour, Vaudeville), PASSING PLACES, THE CHIC NERDS, STONES AND ASHES, EUROPE. Other theatre work includes: MACBETH, A DOLL'S HOUSE (Theatre Babel); MARABOU STORK NIGHTMARES (Citizens', Leicester Haymarket); MARY QUEEN OF SCOTS GOT HER HEAD CHOPPED OFF, KIDNAPPED, CARLUCCO AND THE QUEEN OF HEARTS (Royal Lyceum); DIAL M FOR MURDER (Dundee Rep); LOOT, DRIVING MISS DAISY, CAN'T PAY, WON'T PAY (Byre); ORPHANS (Harbinger); NAE PROBLEM, GOVAN STORIES, JUMP THE LIFE TO COME (7:84); AS YOU LIKE IT, KING LEAR (Oxford Stage Co); GREAT EXPECTATIONS (Lyric, Belfast); JUST FRANK (Theatre Royal, Stratford East). Television and film work includes: CITY CENTRAL, RAB C NESBITT, PUNCH DRUNK, DOUBLE NOUGAT, NERVOUS ENERGY, STRATHBLAIR (BBC); TAGGART, ALBERT AND THE LION (STV); SILENT SCREAM (Antonine Productions); RIFF RAFF (Parallax Pictures).

Pauline Knowles (*Mireille*) For the Traverse: THE SPECULATOR (co-production with Edinburgh International Festival), WIDOWS, THE COLLECTION, MARISOL, KNIVES IN HENS (also with the Bush Theatre). Other theatre work includes: DR LIVINGSTONE, I PRESUME? (Holders Festival, Barbados); MEN SHOULD WEEP (TAG/Dundee Rep); A SCOTS QUAIR (TAG); SWING HAMMER SWING (Citizens'); ELEGIES FOR ANGELS, PUNKS AND RAGING QUEENS (Luckenbooth); TWELFTH NIGHT (Royal Lyceum & Salisbury Theatre) CUTTIN' A RUG, SCHOOL FOR WIVES (Royal Lyceum); ANTIGONE and JUMP, THE LIFE TO COME (7:84); OH WHAT A LOVELY WAR, SHARKS AND CLEANING UP(Wildcat); VODKA AND DAISIES (Annexe); DON JUAN (Penname); ALADDIN (Skint Knees). Television performances include: ACTING WITH RICHARD WILSON, STRATHBLAIR, JOHN BROWN'S BODY. Radio work includes: FLOATING, SUBUTU PASSAGE, WANTIN' A HAND, LEAVE ME ALONE.

Struan Leslie (movement director): Studied at Naropa Institute Colorado and London Contemporary Dance School. Work as Movement Director includes: COSI FAN TUTTI, JENUFA (Welsh National Opera); ORESTEIA (Royal National Theatre); EASY VIRTUE (Chichester); THE MAIDS (Young Vic); ATTEMPTS ON HER LIFE (Teatro Piccolo di Milano); RUMPLESTILTSKIN (Nottingham Playhouse); EASTER, SLAUGHTER CITY, THE MERCHANT OF VENICE; CYRANO DE BERGERAC (RSC); THE RETURN OF THE SOLDIER (Ansuz Theatre Co.); ENDGAME, MORPHIC RESONANCE (Donmar Warehouse); THYESTES (Conspiracy); RHINOCEROS (Riverside Studios); A MIDSUMMER NIGHT'S DREAM (Regent's Park Outdoor Theatre); SPINNING, 10,000 BROKEN MIRRORS (Oval House Theatre); UNTITLED (Conspiracy Theatre). Solo Performances include: NEW CHILD SEXUALITY, GENDERALITY and SEXY GENDER BABY (Chisendale Dance Space, Glasgay '95). He has also directed set pieces in Shakespeare, choreographed musicals and created character movement for theatre, film and television.

Jon Linstrum (lighting designer): Works regularly with Improbable Theatre. Recent lighting designs include SHOCKHEADED PETER (Touring), CINDERELLA, MIDSUMMER NIGHT'S DREAM, DR FAUSTUS, HUNCHBACK OF NOTRE DAME, STICKY (Improbable); A CLOCKWORK ORANGE (Northern Stage); AND NOTHING BUT THE TRUTH (V-Tol Dance Co.); POPCORN (London Apollo); BLAST FROM THE PAST (West Yorkshire Playhouse); IT'S A GREAT BIG SHAME, PARTY GIRLS, THROWAWAY, DICK WITTINGTON (Stratford East). Work as Production Manager includes: BRIGHTON NEW YEAR'S EVE EVENT; OXFORD MILLENNIUM FESTIVAL and ISLINGTON INTERNATIONAL FESTIVAL.

Elizabeth Millbank (*Louise*): Work for the Traverse: AWAY, KORA. Other theatre work includes: Portia in THE MERCHANT OF VENICE (Royal Lyceum); PENNY FOR A SONG (RSC); THE REAL WURLD (Tron); MARY QUEEN OF SCOTS GOT HER HEAD CHOPPED OFF (Perth Rep). Television work includes: THE ANATOMIST, AN ENEMY OF THE PEOPLE, WILLIE ROUGH, THE FATAL SPRING, GOODBYE MR CHIPS (BBC); BOOKIE, THE MACRAME MAN, TAGGART (STV); JOE AND MARY (ANGLIA). Film work includes: THE ROCKING HORSE WINNER (Paramount); THE STRANGER (National Film School).

Colette O'Neil *(Rose):* Appeared as Ines in HUIS CLO, the first production of the Traverse at the old Lawnmarket theatre and in Erust Yandel's AUF DER FREMDE at Edinburgh International Festival. In a long career she has played with the RSC, The National, at the Royal Court, with Theatre Workshop and in the West End. She has appeared in plays and series on TV, most recently in PEAK PRACTICE nad SUNBURN. She has just come from playing Eva in the first play to open the new Soho Theatre in London.

Hope Ross *(Jeannine):* For the Traverse: HIGHLAND SHORTS. Other theatre work includes HOME (Lookout), THE PRINCESS AND THE GOBLIN (MacRobert), KEVIN'S BED (Borderline/Brunton), ALBERTINE IN 5 TIMES and BABYCAKES (Clyde Unity), THE TRICK IS TO KEEP BREATHING (Tron), MEN SHOULD WEEP (TAG/Dundee Rep), I'LL BE SEEING YOU (Brunton), DAMES AT SEA, THE SLAB BOYS and THE SECRET DIARY OF ADRIAN MOLE (Byre). Film work includes: Anna Smith in THE MATCH (Universal), Sadie McGrath in BODYSHIFTERS (Alhambra Films), Miss Dalglish in 3D HALLOWEEN (Telecast International). Television work includes: THE CREATIVES, RECONCILIATION and BAD BOYS (BBC) TAGGART (STV), THE RING OF TRUTH (CH 4).

Ann Scott-Jones *(The Widow):* For the Traverse: PERFECT DAYS (Traverse, Hampstead & tour, Vaudeville), LAZYBED. Other theatre work includes: THE BIG PICTURE by Liz Lochhead (Dundee Rep); RED HOT SHOES, THE MARBLE MADONNA, THE GUID SISTERS (Tron); THE GLASS MENAGERIE, SHINDA THE MAGIC APE (Royal Lyceum); PRECARIOUS LIVING, THE GIN GAME, BRIGHTON BEACH MEMOIRS, STEEL MAGNOLIAS, GASLIGHT, THE MATING GAME (Perth Rep); WITNESS FOR THE PROSECUTION, A FLEA IN HER EAR, ALL MY SONS, THE STEAMIE, DEAR BRUTUS, CAUSE CELEBRE (Pitlochry). Television includes: THE NUCLEAR FAMILY, IT COULD HAPPEN TO ANYBODY, EDGE OF DARKNESS, LET'S SEE, JUTE CITY, BREAKING THE ANGELS BACK, A LIFE IN CHINA, STRATHBLAIR, THE CELTS, THE HIGH LIFE (BBC); THE PRINCESS STALLION, HIGH ROAD, THE PERSONAL TOUCH (STV); JOHN BROWN'S BODY, CLASSIC CHILDREN'S TALES, MILES BETTER (Channel 4). Film work includes: RESTLESS NATIVES, LOCAL HERO, GREYSTOKE, SOFT TOP, HARD SHOULDER, AN ANGEL PASSES BY. Ann has worked extensively in radio, most recently the Woman's Hour serial STILL WATERS, STORYLINE and THE HYDRO.

Ros Steen *(co-director):* Trained: RSAMD. As voice coach for the Traverse: KING OF THE FIELDS, HIGHLAND SHORTS, FAMILY, HERITAGE, KILL THE OLD TORTURE THEIR YOUNG, THE CHIC NERDS, GRETA, LAZYBED, KNIVES IN HENS, PASSING PLACES, BONDAGERS, ROAD TO NIRVANA, SHARP SHORTS, MARISOL, GRACE IN AMERICA, BROTHERS OF THUNDER. Other theatre work includes: OLEANNA, SUMMIT CONFERENCE, KRAPPS'S LAST TAPE, THE DYING GAUL, CONVERSATION WITH A CUPBOARD MAN, EVA PERON, LONG DAY'S JOURNEY INTO NIGHT, (Citizens'); PLAYBOY OF THE WESTERN WORLD, A MIDSUMMER NIGHT'S DREAM (Dundee Rep); SEA URCHINS (Tron & Dundee Rep); HOME, TRANSATLANTIC, THE HANGING TREE, LAUNDRY and ENTERTAINING ANGELS (Lookout); ODYSSEUS THUMP (West Yorkshire Playhouse); MYTHS OF THE NEAR FUTURE (untitled); BEUL

NAM BREUG (Tosg Theatar Gaidhlig); TRAVELS WITH MY AUNT, THE PRICE (Brunton); TRAINSPOTTING (G & J Productions); HOW TO SAY GOODBYE, BABYCAKES (Clyde Unity); ABIGAIL'S PARTY (Perth Rep); LOVERS, PYGMALION, OUR COUNTRY'S GOOD (Royal Lyceum); SUNSET SONG (TAG). Films include: GREGORY'S TWO GIRLS, STELLA DOES TRICKS and STAND AND DELIVER. Television includes: MONARCH OF THE GLEN, HAMISH MACBETH, LOOKING AFTER JOJO, ST ANTHONY'S DAY OFF and CHANGING STEP.

Neil Warmington (designer): Graduated in Fine Art at Maidstone College of Art before attending the post-graduate Theatre Design course at Motley. For the Traverse: KING OF THE FIELDS, FAMILY, PASSING PLACES (TMA Award for Best Design). Theatre credits include: RIDDANCE, CRAZYHORSE (Paines Plough); DON JUAN, TAMING OF THE SHREW (English Touring Theatre); INTIMATE EXCHANGES (Dukes Playhouse, Lancaster); LIFE IS A DREAM (TMA Award Best Design), FIDDLER ON THE ROOF (West Yorkshire Playhouse); THE DUCHESS OF MALFI (Theatre Royal, Bath); DESIRE UNDER THE ELMS, JANE EYRE - Barclays Stage Award for design (Shared Experience); WOMEN LAUGHING (Watford); THE TEMPEST (Contact, Manchester); DISSENT, ANGELS IN AMERICA (7:84); TROILUS AND CRESSIDA (Opera North); HENRY V (Royal Shakespeare Company); MUCH ADO ABOUT NOTHING (Queen's Theatre, London); THE LIFE OF STUFF (Donmar Warehouse); WAITING FOR GODOT, MUCH ADO ABOUT NOTHING (Liverpool Everyman); COMEDIANS, MERLIN (Parts 1& 2) (Royal Lyceum). Neil is currently designing THE MARRIAGE OF FIGARO for Garsington Opera Festival and designed the launch of Glasgow's Year of Architecture 1999. He has also won The Linbury Prize for stage design and The Sir Alfred Munnings Florence prize for painting.

Solemn Mass for a Full Moon in Summer is supported with assistance from the Office of the Government of Québec, London and the Canadian High Commission, London.

For generous help on
Solemn Mass for a Full Moon in Summer
the Traverse thanks:

The Christina Mary Hendrie Trust for
Scottish and Canadian Charities

LEVER BROTHERS for wardrobe care

Sets, props and costumes for
Solemn Mass for a Full Moon in Summer
created by Traverse Workshops
(funded by the National Lottery)

Kevin Low *production photography*
Euan Myles *print photography*

TRAVERSE THEATRE

One of the most important theatres in Britain The Observer

Edinburgh's **Traverse Theatre** is Scotland's new writing theatre, with a 37 year record of excellence. With quality, award-winning productions and programming, the Traverse receives accolades at home and abroad from audiences and critics alike.

The Traverse has an unrivalled reputation for producing contemporary theatre of the highest quality, invention and energy, commissioning and supporting writers from Scotland and around the world and facilitating numerous script development workshops, rehearsed readings and public writing workshops. The Traverse aims to produce several major new theatre productions plus a Scottish touring production each year. It is unique in Scotland in its exclusive dedication to new writing, providing the infrastructure, professional support and expertise to ensure the development of a sustainable and relevant theatre culture for Scotland and the UK.

Traverse Theatre Company productions have been seen worldwide including London, Toronto, Budapest and New York. Recent touring successes in Scotland include PERFECT DAYS by Liz Lochhead, PASSING PLACES by Stephen Greenhorn, HIGHLAND SHORTS, HERITAGE by Nicola McCartney and LAZYBED by Iain Crichton Smith. PERFECT DAYS also played the Vaudeville Theatre in London's West End in 1999.

The Traverse can be relied upon to produce more good-quality new plays than any other Fringe venue Daily Telegraph

During the Edinburgh Festival the Traverse is one of the most important venues with world class premieres playing daily in the two theatre spaces. The Traverse regularly wins awards at the Edinburgh Festival Fringe, including recent *Scotsman Fringe Firsts* for Traverse productions KILL THE OLD TORTURE THEIR YOUNG by David Harrower and PERFECT DAYS by Liz Lochhead.

An essential element of the Traverse Company's activities takes place within the educational sector, concentrating on the process of playwriting for young people. The Traverse flagship education project CLASS ACT offers young people in schools the opportunity to work with theatre professionals and see their work performed on the Traverse stage. In addition the Traverse Young Writers group, led by professional playwrights, has been running for over three years and meets weekly.

SPONSORSHIP

Sponsorship income enables the Traverse to commission and produce new plays and offer audiences a diverse and exciting programme of events throughout the year.
We would like to thank the following companies for their support throughout the year:

BANK OF SCOTLAND

B B C Scotland

E S P C

CORPORATE ASSOCIATE SCHEME

LEVEL ONE
Balfour Beatty
Scottish Life the PENSION company
United Distillers & Vintners

LEVEL TWO
Laurence Smith -
Wine Merchants
NB Information
Willis Corroon Scotland Ltd
Wired Nomad

LEVEL THREE
Alistir Tait FGA -
Antiques & Fine Jewellery
Nicholas Groves Raines -
Architects
McCabe Partnership -
Chartered Accountants
KPMG
Scottish Post Office Board

With thanks to

Navy Blue Design, print designers for the Traverse and George Stewarts the printers.

Purchase of the Traverse Box Office, computer network and technical and training equipment has been made possible with money from The Scottish Arts Council National Lottery Fund.

THE SCOTTISH ARTS COUNCIL
National Lottery Fund

The Traverse Theatre's work would not be possible without the support of

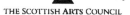
THE SCOTTISH ARTS COUNCIL
·EDINBVRGH·
THE CITY OF EDINBURGH COUNCIL

The Traverse receives financial assistance for its educational and development work from

John Lewis Partnership, Peggy Ramsay Foundation, Binks Trust, The Yapp Charitable Trusts, The Bulldog Prinsep Theatrical Trust, Calouste Gulbenkian Foundation, Gannochy Trust, Gordon Fraser Charitable Trust, The Garfield Weston Foundation.

The Education Institute of Scotland, supporting arts projects produced by and for children. **EIS**

Charity No. SC002368

"A stunning programme of theatre" THE GUARDIAN

For six months each year the Barbican Centre plays host to a selection of the very finest in drama, dance and music theatre from all corners of the globe. The two annual BITE festivals to date have presented a startling variety of work that is new, fresh, challenging and entertaining - resulting in several Olivier and Peter Brook Award nominations. Our most recent accolade was the International Theatre Institute Award for BITE:99's dance programme.

In 1998 America was the predominant focus; last year we enjoyed highly acclaimed festivals devoted to St Petersburg and to the complete stage works of Samuel Beckett (a collaboration with the **Gate Theatre Dublin**). This May sees the launch of BITE:00, a third adventurous programme of UK and London premieres, in which world-famous companies will be seen alongside artists new to Britain. The season opens fittingly with this first BITE/Traverse Theatre Company co-production. Other highlights to follow include **Laurie Anderson**'s multi-media interpretation of Melville's **Moby Dick**, the eagerly anticipated return of Chicago's **Steppenwolf Theatre Company** and of the **Merce Cunningham Dance Company** with another BITE co-commission, the renowned **Comédie-Française** in Molière, and the **Abbey Theatre Dublin**'s acclaimed production of **The Secret Fall of Constance Wilde**. Meanwhile, in the more intimate setting of the Pit Theatre, we present an exciting range of work from Australia, America, Trinidad and Tobago, France, Bulgaria and Ireland.

That is the excitement of BITE. Each year something old, something new - but never, we trust, entirely what you expect. Join us.

Graham Sheffield
Artistic Director
Barbican Centre

MAY TO OCTOBER 2000

SOLEMN MASS FOR
A FULL MOON IN SUMMER
TRAVERSE THEATRE COMPANY
17 May to 3 June

SONGS AND STORIES FROM
MOBY DICK
LAURIE ANDERSON
24 to 28 May

SCAPIN'S TRICKERY
LA COMÉDIE FRANÇAISE
7 to 14 June

THE TRAGIC FLUTE
THE BELLBOYS
10, 11 & 24 June

LE JARDIN IO IO ITO ITO
COMPAGNIE MONTALVO-HERVIEU
20 to 24 June

THE OVERCOAT
CREDO THEATRE
21 June to 1 July

BOX THE PONY/
WHITE BAPTIST ABBA FAN
HEADS UP AUSTRALIAN ARTS 100
4 to 8 July

JET LAG
**THE BUILDERS ASSOCIATION AND
DILLER + SCOFIDIO**
5 to 8 July

I'LL GO ON
THE GATE THEATRE DUBLIN
12 to 29 July

MIX
**COMPANHIA DE DANÇA
DEBORAH COLKER**
18 to 22 July

ONE FLEW OVER
THE CUCKOO'S NEST
**STEPPENWOLF
THEATRE COMPANY**
27 July to 5 August

CLEAR WATER
OVAL HOUSE
23 August to 9 September

EXCENTRICUS
CIRQUE ÉLOIZE
24 August to 2 September

LA DANSE DU TEMPS
BALLET ATLANTIQUE
6 to 9 September

PARALLEL LINES
THEATRE CRYPTIC
13 to 23 September

THE SECRET FALL
OF CONSTANCE WILDE
THE ABBEY THEATRE DUBLIN
27 September to 7 October

KWAIDAN
PING CHONG AND COMPANY
27 September to 7 October

BIPED
**MERCE CUNNINGHAM
DANCE COMPANY**
10 to 14 October

To book tickets, please call the Barbican Centre Box Office on **020 7638 8891**

Please make sure that digital watch alarms and mobile phones are switched off during the performance. In accordance with the requirements of the licensing authority, sitting or standing in any gangway is not permitted. No smoking, eating or drinking is allowed in the auditorium. No cameras, tape recorders or any other recording equipment may be taken into the hall.

 **Barbican Centre** The Barbican Centre is owned, funded and managed by the Corporation of London

SOLEMN MASS FOR A FULL MOON IN SUMMER

(Messe solennelle pour une pleine lune d'été)

by
Michel Tremblay

Translated by Martin Bowman and Bill Findlay,
who dedicate this translation to
Gillian Horgan and Jessica Burns

Ce que je voulais dire, c'est que de même que la messe
est un acte qui existe sur plusieurs plans, pas sur un seul,
de même un grand amour partagé par deux êtres peut avoir
une importance par-delà le monde connu de nous.

(What I mean is that, just as the mass is an act which exists
on several planes, not on one only, so a great love shared
by two beings can have an importance beyond
the world known by us.)

John Cowper Powys
Les Enchantements de Glastonbury
(Glastonbury Romance)

A Nick Hern Book

Solemn Mass for a Full Moon in Summer first published
in Great Britain in 2000 by Nick Hern Books, 14 Larden Road,
London W3 7ST, in association with the Traverse Theatre,
Edinburgh

Typeset by Country Setting, Kingsdown, Kent CT14 8ES
Printed in Great Britain by Athenaeum Press Ltd, Gateshead

A CIP catalogue record for this book is available from the
British Library

ISBN 185459 495 8

The Mass

Characters

ISABELLE, *in her early twenties*

YANNICK, *in his early twenties*

JEANNINE, *in her fifties*

LOUISE, *in her fifties*

ROSE, *in her early sixties*

MATHIEU, *in his late thirties*

GASTON, *in his sixties*

MIREILLE, *in her early forties*

YVON, *in his fifties*

GÉRARD, *in his fifties*

THE WIDOW, *in her fifties*

Notes

Separate speeches or parts of speeches that appear within square brackets indicate that the characters speak those lines simultaneously. Vertical lines in the margin indicate passages that are to be repeated a number of times.

This text went to press before the end of rehearsals, so may differ from the play as performed.

I

INTROIT

The facades of two houses somewhere in the Plateau Mont-Royal [in Montreal]. It is a full moon in the month of August; the weather is hot, humid, heavy. (Sketch: Michel Tremblay.)

Slowly, THE ELEVEN CHARACTERS *come out on to the balconies.*

THE WIDOW (*ground floor right*) *sits on a rocking chair;* ROSE (*second floor left*) *sits on a chair which her son* MATHIEU *carries out.*

ISABELLE *and* YANNICK (*top floor left*) *kiss.*

YVON (*ground floor left*) *sits down on the steps to the balcony while his friend* GÉRARD *comes out, leaning on a cane.*

MIREILLE (*second floor right*) *sits down on the top step of the external stairs, directly in front of the door to the internal stairs leading to* JEANNINE *and* LOUISE*'s flat.*

GASTON, *her father, stands very erect in the corner of the balcony as if he wanted to rule the whole neighbourhood.* GASTON *has lost both his forearms in a work accident.*

JEANNINE *and* LOUISE (*top floor right*) *are leaning on the wooden railing of their balcony. Their shoulders are touching, but they are not looking at each other.*

Nobody speaks.

They seem to be waiting for something.

The silence before the ceremony must be heavy, almost oppressive.

II

KYRIE

lento

THE ELEVEN CHARACTERS (*in unison, very precisely*).
   My God. My God. My God. It's lovely. My God, it's lovely.

THE WIDOW. It's that

[lovely.

ROSE. It is . . .]

it's that . . .

[lovely.

JEANNINE and LOUISE. It is . . .]

it's so lovely!

ROSE. No a single cloud . . .

THE WIDOW. Hardly a braith ae air . . .

LOUISE. It's close . . . I like it when it's close . . .

JEANNINE. It's stifling . . . the word is stifling.

LOUISE. If you say so . . . But I like it when it's stifling.

   Silence.

ISABELLE. Hey, look at that.

THE OTHER CHARACTERS. My God.

ISABELLE. That's a weird light.

THE WIDOW. Wid make ye feel ye waantit tae . . .

THE WIDOW, JEANNINE, LOUISE. . . . sleep outside.

ISABELLE. It goat dark aw ae a sudden, ye couldnae see
   nothin, and then . . .

THE ELEVEN CHARACTERS. My God.

ISABELLE. . . . it's turnin pure white.

LOUISE. I'd like it to be like this all year . . .

Silence.

THE WIDOW. Sometimes we done that, me'n George, before . . .

JEANNINE. Set up a hammock . . .

LOUISE. . . . like we did

[before . . .

THE WIDOW. . . . before. . . .]

he passed away . . .

[. . . we'd settle wirsels oan the back-balcony

JEANNINE, LOUISE. . . . we'd set up a hammock here, hang
    blankets . . .]

THE WIDOW, JEANNINE, LOUISE . . . so's the neighbours
    couldn't see us . . . [WIDOW *says 'couldnae'.*]

LOUISE. . . . then we slept as we swayed.

ROSE. We'd be there thegither aw night long.

[THE WIDOW, JEANNINE, LOUISE We were so happy.

ROSE. We'd be so happy.]

[JEANNINE, LOUISE. The two of us.

THE WIDOW, ROSE. The two ae us.]

LOUISE. Weren't we? Weren't we?

Silence.

YANNICK. It's the moon comin! It's the moon comin! That's
    how it's white like this.

ISABELLE, YANNICK, JEANNINE, LOUISE, ROSE,
    THE WIDOW. My God.

MATHIEU, GASTON, MIREILLE, YVON, GÉRARD. My
    God.

Silence.

GÉRARD. It's really lovely, but this heat . . .

YVON. No be possible, eh no?

GÉRARD. No. No. Up till last year it woulda been possible, but now . . .

ISABELLE, YANNICK. No be long till it's oot.

THE WIDOW. An auld mattress . . .

[ISABELLE, YANNICK. That's how it's white like this.

THE WIDOW. That's how the mood jist took us . . .]

[ISABELLE, YANNICK. No be long till it's oot.

THE WIDOW. That's how the mood jist took us . . .]

GÉRARD. It's really, really lovely . . .

[YVON. Ah know . . .

MIREILLE. Ye need somethin?]

[GÉRARD. No, you don't know.

GASTON. No, ah need nothin.]

THE WIDOW, JEANNINE, LOUISE. We slept like logs.

THE WIDOW. It seems no that long ago.

Silence.

MATHIEU. To think I was doin that no long ago . . . Fool that I was . . .

THE ELEVEN CHARACTERS (*quietly*). My God.

MATHIEU. Sleepin . . . like that . . . outside.

ROSE. Don't think aboot that . . .

[YANNICK. Know whit we should dae?

ROSE. Don't think aboot that . . .]

[ISABELLE. Ah seen this comin, you! Ah seen it comin since we wir eatin . . .

YANNICK. We should drag the mattress oot oantae the balcony . . .

THE WIDOW, JEANNINE, LOUISE. We never noticed the night passing.

ROSE. It's too lovely a night tae be thinkin aboot things like that.

MATHIEU. Aye . . . forget everythin . . . then sleep.

MIREILLE. Ye shair ye need nothin?

YVON. Ye like me tae bring oot a chair?]

[GASTON, GÉRARD No, ah need nothin.

ISABELLE. Ah seen you comin on tae me, gantin fur it . . .

YANNICK. We could hing up blankets. Tae stoap the neighbours seein us . . .

JEANNINE, LOUISE (*not together. LOUISE begins on JEANNINE's 'once'*.) I never woke up even once . . .

MATHIEU. Escape intae sleep, forget everythin, wipe it all out . . .

GASTON. Ah need nothin. Ah'm fine as ah am.

GÉRARD. Ah need nothin. Ah'm no a cripple.

THE WIDOW. The haill night ah nivir woke up wance even . . .]

MATHIEU. Wipe it all out. Once and for all.

THE ELEVEN CHARACTERS (*very loud*). My God.

THE WIDOW. Have mercy upon me.

[MATHIEU. Have mercy upon me.

THE WIDOW. Ah'm no able tae . . .]

MATHIEU. I'm not able to . . .

[ISABELLE. You're no subtle when yir feelin that wey.

YANNICK. You ivir done it in the moonlight?]

[YANNICK. Subtle?

THE WIDOW Ah'm no able tae.

MATHIEU. I'm not able to.]

YANNICK. How wid ah be subtle?

ROSE, YVON. Ah don't like it when you're in this mood. Ye sure ah kin do nothin?

[JEANNINE. That's all in the past.

LOUISE. All finished and done with.]

The following choral lines are given three times.

ISABELLE. But deep doon ah love it when you prowl roond me, comin on tae me, excitin me, excitin me . . .

YANNICK. But deep doon you love it when ah prowl roond ye, sweet-talkin, sweet-talkin . . .

JEANNINE. After twenty-five years we don't feel like doing those kind of things, sad to say . . .

LOUISE. How is it things like that go away and don't come back? I don't understand. I don't understand . . .

ROSE. Ah know there's nothin ah kin do, ah'm sorry . . . But ah feel ah'm that helpless . . .

MATHIEU. I can't go on livin like this . . . I've got tae do somethin . . .

GASTON. If ah need somethin, ah'll let ye know . . . Wait till ah tell ye, will ye! Wait!

MIREILLE. Excuse me! . . . Think ah don't know ye cannae abide me waantin tae help ye? . . . Ah know it only too well!

YVON. Ah know you're no a cripple, ah'm no implyin that, stupid!

GÉRARD. As long as ah'm able tae manage fur maself ah'll do it maself, thank you!

THE WIDOW. Ah cannae abide livin like this . . . Ah've goat tae dae somethin . . .

[ISABELLE. Ah like it when yir eyes chynge colour and yir smile chynges its meanin . . .

YANNICK. You like it when ma eyes chynge colour and ma
smile chynges its meanin. . . .]

THE WIDOW. My God.

MATHIEU. My God.

GÉRARD. My God.

THE WIDOW, MATHIEU, GÉRARD. Have mercy upon me.

Silence.

YANNICK. Will we dae it?

ISABELLE. You're wild!

YANNICK. Will we dae it?

ISABELLE. You're wild!

YANNICK. Will we dae it?

ISABELLE. You're wild!

[YANNICK. Will we dae it?

THE WIDOW, MATHIEU, GÉRARD. My God.]

[ISABELLE. You're wild!

THE WIDOW, MATHIEU, GÉRARD. Have mercy upon me.]

[YANNICK. Will we dae it?

MATHIEU. Christ.]

[ISABELLE. You're wild!

THE WIDOW, GÉRARD. My God.]

[YANNICK. Will we dae it?

MATHIEU, GÉRARD. Christ.]

[YANNICK. Will we dae it?

THE WIDOW, MATHIEU, GÉRARD. Christ.]

[ISABELLE. You're wild!

THE WIDOW. Dear Christ.]

[YANNICK. Will we dae it?

THE WIDOW, MATHIEU, GÉRARD. Christ.]

[ISABELLE. You're wild!

THE WIDOW, MATHIEU, GÉRARD. Have mercy upon me.]

[YANNICK. Will we dae it?

THE WIDOW, MATHIEU, GÉRARD. Have mercy upon me.]

[ISABELLE. You're wild!

THE WIDOW, MATHIEU, GÉRARD. Have mercy upon me.]

[YANNICK. Will we dae it?

THE WIDOW, MATHIEU, GÉRARD. Have mercy upon me.]

[ISABELLE. You're wild!

THE WIDOW, MATHIEU, GÉRARD. Have mercy upon me.]

YANNICK. Will we dae it?

ISABELLE. You're wild!

YANNICK. Will we dae it?

ISABELLE. You're wild!

YANNICK. Will we dae it?

ISABELLE. Awright!

Silence.

YVON. Is it no time for yir pills?

GÉRARD. Yes of course it's time for ma pills.

YVON. So, what are ye waitin fur?

GÉRARD. Ah don't know.

YVON. What are ye waitin fur?

GÉRARD. Ah don't know.

YVON. If yir late in takin them . . .

GÉRARD. Aye, aye, ah know . . . They dinnae take effect,
or they take too much ae an effect, or they hiv the wrong

effect . . . If ah took them aw at the same time, though, that wid hiv the right effect awright!

MATHIEU. Christ.

THE WIDOW. Christ.

GÉRARD. Christ.

THE WIDOW, MATHIEU, GÉRARD. Have mercy upon me.

[ISABELLE. Ah like it when yir eyes chynge colour then yir smile chynges its meanin . . .

YANNICK. You like it when ma eyes chynge colour then ma smile chynges its meanin . . .]

Silence.

YANNICK (*quietly, until* MIREILLE *and* ISABELLE *say 'awright'*). Will we dae it?

ISABELLE (*quietly, until the moment she says 'awright' with* MIREILLE). You're wild!

MIREILLE. Ah promise ah'll no be late back . . .

GASTON. You didnae tell me ye wur gaun oot.

MIREILLE. Ah did so.

GASTON. You did not.

MIREILLE. Ah did so tell ye!

GASTON. You did not tell me!

MIREILLE. Ah tellt ye at the tea-table but you wurnae listenin . . .

GASTON. You did not tell me!

MIREILLE. Well, ah'm tellin ye noo. Ah'm gaun oot! And ah'm tellin ye anaw ah'll no be late back. If yir needin nothin as ye say, then ah'm leavin right this minute.

GASTON. But ma bed?

MIREILLE. Yir no needin yir bed right noo.

GASTON. Ma faced waashed?

MIREILLE. It'll be hoors afore you're in yir bed . . . In the summer-time, if thurs a full moon, it's guaranteed you'll stey oot oan the balcony the haill night. When ah wis wee, ma pals wur shair ye wur a werewolf.

GASTON. Supposin ah need somethin and you're no here . . .

MIREILLE. Ye tellt me ye needed nuhin.

GASTON. Ah'm needin nuhin the noo, but . . .

[MIREILLE. Awright . . .

ISABELLE. Awright!]

MIREILLE. . . . awright, ah'll stey!

[ISABELLE. Ah like it when yir eyes chynge colour then yir smile chynges its meanin . . .

YANNICK. You like it when ma eyes chynge colour then ma smile chynges its meanin . . .

MIREILLE. Ah'll stey! Fur aw ah wis gaunnae dae anyhow . . . fur aw ah wis gaunnae dae! Christ, am ah no scunnert!]

THE WIDOW, MATHIEU, MIREILLE, YVON, GÉRARD. Christ! Have mercy upon me!

Silence.

JEANNINE. Jesus, what's with the long face? It's a lovely night, and you're supposed to like it when it's 'close' like this . . .

JEANNINE, ROSE. Jesus . . .

ROSE. . . . ah don't know what tae do, ah don't know what tae say tae snap ye oot yir mood . . .

JEANNINE, ROSE. Jesus.

GASTON. Christ.

[LOUISE. Yes, it is lovely . . .

MATHIEU. You don't need to say anythin . . .

THE WIDOW (*quietly*). Have mercy upon me . . .]

[GASTON. Ye'll make me feel ah'm bein selfish again . . .

GÉRARD (*quietly*). Have mercy upon me . . .]

[MIREILLE. And so ye ur!

THE WIDOW (*quietly*). Christ.]

[GASTON. Ah'm no bein selfish!

GÉRARD (*quietly*). Christ.]

[MIREILLE. Christ, no selfish!

THE WIDOW (*quietly*). Have mercy upon me.]

[GASTON. When've ah ivir been selfish wi ye, eh?

GÉRARD (*quietly*). Have mercy upon us.]

[MIREILLE. When?

THE WIDOW (*quietly*). Christ.]

[GASTON. When, eh?

GÉRARD (*quietly*). Christ.]

[MIREILLE. Need ye ask when?

THE WIDOW (*quietly*). Have mercy upon me.]

[GASTON (*quietly*). When?

GÉRARD. Christ.]

[MIREILLE. You really waantin me tae go back ower ma haill life fur ye?! Jesus!

THE WIDOW, GÉRARD (*quietly, and slowly so that the three 'Jesus' are said at the same time*). Have mercy upon me, Jesus.]

MIREILLE. Everythin ah dae, every single thing ah dae in ma life is done fur you. Ma haill life is gien ower tae you, yet you show no a bit ae gratitude. No wan measly bit! Wid you no say that wis selfish?

Silence.

JEANNINE. Nothing to say?

MATHIEU. I'll spend ma life alone . . .

JEANNINE. Nothing to say?

MATHIEU. I'll spend ma life alone, I suppose . . .

LOUISE. It's not always enough that the weather's lovely,
y'know. . .

JEANNINE. Meaning what?

LOUISE. Nothing . . . nothing . . .

JEANNINE. Meaning what exactly? The full moon isn't
enough for you tonight? It being 'close' like this isn't
enough?

LOUISE. Och, leave it. I don't feel like discussing it . . .

JEANNINE. Jesus! For you not to want to talk!

LOUISE. I don't feel like discussing it, that's all. It's not
complicated!

JEANNINE. For you not to want to talk . . .

JEANNINE, LOUISE, ROSE, MATHIEU, GASTON,
MIREILLE, YVON, GÉRARD, THE WIDOW. Jesus.

MIREILLE. Am ah supposed tae stey here suffocatin?

[YANNICK. Will we dae it?

THE OTHERS. Jesus.]

[ISABELLE. Awright!

THE OTHERS (*except* YANNICK). Have mercy upon me.]

THE NINE OTHERS (*during which* YANNICK *and*
ISABELLE *go out*). Have mercy upon me.

THE WIDOW. It's ma furst full moon . . .

[MATHIEU. It's ma . . .

THE WIDOW. Withoot him . . .]

[MATHIEU. . . . first full moon . . .

THE WIDOW. It's ma. . . .]

[MATHIEU. . . . without him.

THE WIDOW. . . . furst full moon . . .]

*They continue in the same rhythm during the exchange
between* LOUISE *and* JEANNINE.

LOUISE. Even if I explained it to you, you wouldn't
understand . . .

JEANNINE. Oh yes, tell me I never understand anything but
you always do. Jesus!

LOUISE. I never said you never understood anything . . .

JEANNINE. Yes you did!

LOUISE. I did not!

JEANNINE. Yes you did! I've known you long enough to
know what you mean when you speak to me.

LOUISE. Well, if you're so clever, I won't need to speak.
You'll know in advance what I'm going to say. How bother
even speaking?

JEANNINE. I hate it when you act smart like that.

LOUISE. I'm not acting smart.

JEANNINE. Shut up then!

LOUISE. Make your mind up. D'you want me to shut up or
d'you want me to speak?

JEANNINE. Shut up! Please, pretty please!

LOUISE. Oh, aye . . . then if I don't say anything for a while
you'll turn round and criticise me for not speaking!

JEANNINE. I've told you to shut it! You want a skelp?!

LOUISE. Oh yes, it always comes round to that . . .

JEANNINE. Shut it!

LOUISE. Oh yes . . .

JEANNINE. Shut it!

LOUISE. Oh yes . . . oh yes . . . oh yes . . .

JEANNINE, LOUISE. Jesus Christ!

[THE WIDOW. It's ma furst full moon withoot him.

MATHIEU. It's ma first full moon without him.]

THE NINE CHARACTERS. Lord, have mercy upon me.

[THE WIDOW. It dis nae guid thinkin aboot it.

MATHIEU. It does no good thinkin about it.]

THE WIDOW. It's done wi.

MATHIEU. It's done with.

The following lines are repeated nine times in crescendo.

JEANNINE. If you've nothing more to say to me, then shut it!

LOUISE. Your wish is my command. My lips are silent.

ROSE. Ah do what ah kin tae help ye, ah do what ah kin . . .

MATHIEU. It does no good thinkin about it, it's done with.

GASTON. If ah need somethin, ah'll tell ye.

MIREILLE. Ah'll stey wi ye, ah'll stey in.

YVON. Ah do what ah can tae help ye, ah do what ah can.

GÉRARD. If ah need somethin, ah'll tell ye.

THE WIDOW. It dis nae guid thinkin aboot it, it's finished and done wi.

THE NINE CHARACTERS (*twice, very loud*). My God! Christ! Lord! HAVE MERCY UPON US!

III

EXULTATE JUBILATE

allegro vivace

ISABELLE *and* YANNICK *come out of their flat through the door which gives on to the side of* ROSE *and* MATHIEU*'s balcony.*

ISABELLE. It's too early, that's aw. Let's go fur a walk . . .

ROSE. Good evenin . . .

ISABELLE. Oh . . . good evenin . . .

MATHIEU, YANNICK. Good evenin.

ISABELLE *and* YANNICK *go down the stairs almost running.*

ISABELLE. See . . . Ye cannae breathe but everybody knows aboot it . . . They're aw oot oan thur balconies . . . We'll go fur a walk then take the mattress and blankets oot later . . .

YANNICK. How no take thum oot oan the back balcony?

ISABELLE. Wance you git somethin in yir heid, you! Ah've tellt ye ten times in the last five minutes: because it's no nice oan the back balcony. Are you scoobied or whit? If wur gonnae sleep under the stars, we'll dae it at the front, where there're trees, where it smells nice, and where we kin see the full moon! You've been harpin oan aboot it fur three days. Surely ye kin wait a bit longer fur a snog?

YANNICK. It'll no be a snog!

ISABELLE. Aw the mair reason tae wait till they've went tae bed. Ah prefer daein it when we've the place tae oorselves, wi jist the moon above us. Ah don't waant the neighbours hearin us moanin.

YANNICK. You squealin, ye mean!

ISABELLE. Big heid!

YANNICK. You'll no care if yir oan the back balcony or the front balcony, ye'll be too busy tae notice . . .

ISABELLE (*mocking*). Too busy daein whit? Countin the stars?

YANNICK. At the full moon, men turn intae werewolves . . .

ISABELLE (*laughing*). At the full moon, men turn intae pigs, pure and simple.

YANNICK. Are ye complainin?

ISABELLE. Ah nivir said that.

YANNICK. Will we dae it?

ISABELLE. You're wild!

YANNICK. Will we dae it?

ISABELLE. Quit it, will ye . . .

YANNICK. Will we dae it . . .

ISABELLE. Quit it . . .

They kiss.

YVON. It's been a long time since we had that problem, eh?

GÉRARD (*smiling*). We were like that?

YVON. You've a shoart memory . . .

GÉRARD. A shoart memory? Even supposin ah could remember, it was a helluva long time ago!

MIREILLE. It's nice tae see thum like that . . .

LOUISE. It's nice to see them like that . . .

THE WIDOW. It's nice tae see thum like that . . .

YVON. It's nice tae see you . . .

ISABELLE. Sorry if we're talkin too loud . . .

YVON. Not at all . . . It's no *that* yese do too loud . . .

ISABELLE. Youse're waitin fur the full moon as well?

YVON *and* GÉRARD *look at each other.*

YVON. Aye. That's right. We're waitin fur the full moon as well . . .

YANNICK. Look . . . there's it . . .

MIREILLE. Where's it?

YANNICK. There, look, between the branches . . .

ROSE. Oh, aye . . .

JEANNINE. Oh . . .

YVON. Oh, aye . . .

LOUISE. Oh . . .

GASTON. Look at that . . . worth the waitin fur!

THE WIDOW. Anither lonely widow . . .

GÉRARD. Oh, aye . . .

MATHIEU. I'm sorry . . . I can't look at it . . .

ROSE. Dinnae go . . . you'll feel worse if yir jist yirsel . . .

ISABELLE. Ye'd think it came oot the tree; like a red fruit the tree wis offerin us . . .

YANNICK. Ma dad always said the full moon turnt him wild . . .

[. . . wild like a werewolf in heat!

ISABELLE. Ma mum always said . . .]

. . . the full moon turnt her wild . . .

[. . . wild like a she-wolf in heat!

YANNICK. He ran roond the hoose howlin . . .]

. . . like a wolf . . .

ISABELLE. She ran roond the hoose howlin . . .

[. . . like a she-wolf . . .

YANNICK. He pawed ma mum . . .]

[. . . in ivry room and cupboard . . .

ISABELLE. She pawed ma dad . . .]

. . . in ivry room and cupboard . . .

YANNICK. While us kids . . .

[. . . watched oan . . .

ISABELLE. While us kids . . .]

[. . . watched oan . . .

YANNICK. While us kids . . .]

[. . . watched oan . . .

ISABELLE. While us kids . . .]

. . . watched oan . . .

YANNICK. . . . we didnae understand but we couldnae wait . . .

[tae be their age . . .

ISABELLE. . . . we didnae understand . . .]

. . . but we couldnae wait tae be their age . . .

ISABELLE, YANNICK. . . . so's tae dae the same thing! Dae the same thing as them!

[JEANNINE, LOUISE. It's nice to see them like that.

GASTON, MIREILLE, ROSE. It's nice tae see thum like that.

YVON, GÉRARD. We don't hiv that problem any longer . . .

THE WIDOW. Ah cannae look at them . . .

MATHIEU. I can't look at them . . .

ISABELLE. The full moon his the same effect oan me as oan ma mum!

YANNICK. The full moon his the same effect oan me as oan ma dad!]

[ISABELLE. The full moon his the same effect oan me as oan ma mum!

YANNICK. The full moon his the same effect oan me as oan ma dad!]

ISABELLE. Ma skin tells me when the full moon is comin . . .

YANNICK. Ma skin tells me when the full moon is comin . . .

ISABELLE. Ma heart tells me when the full moon is comin . . .

YANNICK. Ma heart tells me when the full moon is comin . . .

ISABELLE. . . . ma blood heats up . . .

YANNICK. . . . ma blood heats up . . .

ISABELLE. . . . ma senses heat up . . .

YANNICK. . . . ma senses heat up . . .

ISABELLE. . . . and it's no jist . . .

[. . . sometimes ah want ye . . .

YANNICK. . . . and it's no jist sometimes ah want ye . . .]

ISABELLE, YANNICK. . . . it's aw the time, ivrywhere, always!

[ISABELLE. The full moon his the same effect oan me as oan ma mum!

YANNICK. The full moon his the same effect oan me as oan ma dad!

JEANNINE, LOUISE. It's nice to see them like that.

GASTON, MIREILLE, ROSE. It's nice tae see thum like that.

YVON, GÉRARD. We don't hiv that problem any longer . . .

THE WIDOW. Ah cannae look at them . . .

MATHIEU. I can't look at them . . .]

ISABELLE. Look! The red fruit . . .

[. . . above the tree!

YANNICK. Look! The red fruit . . .]

. . . above the tree!

ISABELLE. Quick!

YANNICK. Quick!

ISABELLE. Quick!

YANNICK. Quick! Let's go upstairs.

ISABELLE. No!

YANNICK. Let's go upstairs! Now! . . .

ISABELLE. Let's no!

YANNICK. Let's dae it right here . . .

ISABELLE. Let's dae it right here . . .

YANNICK. Let's forget the balconies . . .

ISABELLE. Let's forget the balconies . . .

YANNICK. Let's forget the neighbours . . .

ISABELLE. Let's forget the neighbours . . .

YANNICK. Ma blood's heatin up!

ISABELLE. Ma blood's heatin up!

YANNICK. Ah'm in heat!

ISABELLE. Ah'm in heat!

YANNICK. Ah feel like howlin, like . . .

> *The following phrases given simultaneously by* YANNICK
> *and* ISABELLE *are said three times.*

[. . . a werewolf!

ISABELLE. Ah feel like howlin . . .]

. . . like a she-werewolf!

YANNICK. Like a he-werewolf!

ISABELLE. Like a she-werewolf!

YANNICK. Like a he-werewolf!

ISABELLE. Like a she-werewolf!

YANNICK. The tree has flung the moon intae the sky . . .

[. . . like an orange of love!

ISABELLE. The tree has flung the moon intae the sky . . .]

. . . like an orange of love!

YANNICK. Ah want ye!

ISABELLE. Ah want ye!

YANNICK. Ah want ye!

ISABELLE. Ah want ye!

YANNICK. Ah want ye oan the stairs!

ISABELLE. Oan the stairs!

YANNICK. Oan the livin-room rug!

ISABELLE. Oan the livin-room rug!

YANNICK. Oan the kitchen-table!

ISABELLE. Oan the kitchen-table!

YANNICK. In the shower!

ISABELLE. Yes, yes, in the shower!

YANNICK. In the bath!

ISABELLE. In the bath!

YANNICK. In bed, again and again!

ISABELLE. And again, if ye want!

YANNICK. Ah want you in the kitchen between the kettle and the microwave!

ISABELLE. Ah want you oan the bathroom flair between the pan and the lavvie brush!

YANNICK. Ah want you ootside, oan the roof, oan the balcony!

ISABELLE. Ah want you ootside oan the balcony, under the orange ae love, above the neighbours listenin tae us moanin!

YANNICK. Ah want you at the front and at the back!

ISABELLE. Ah want you at the back and at the front!

YANNICK. Ah want you in heaven and in hell!

ISABELLE. Ah want you hellishly in hell!

YANNICK. Ah want you!

ISABELLE. Ah want you!

YANNICK. Ah want you!

ISABELLE. Ah want you! Ah want you in the wardrobe!

YANNICK. In the wardrobe!

ISABELLE. Ah want you in the fridge!

YANNICK. In the fridge!

ISABELLE. Ah want you under the sink!

YANNICK. You're nuts!

ISABELLE. Ah want you under the sink!

YANNICK. Thurs no enough room!

ISABELLE. Ah want you under the sink!

YANNICK. Okay! Under the sink!

ISABELLE. Ah want you hangin aff the curtains! Ah want you
    rolled up in the rug! Ah want you tied tae the hoover!

YANNICK. Ah want you ivrywhere ye fancy!

ISABELLE. Ah want you ivrywhere!

YANNICK. Ah want you ivrywhere!

ISABELLE. Ah want you at the front and at the back!

YANNICK. Ah want you at the back and at the front!

ISABELLE. Ah want you in heaven and in hell!

YANNICK. Ah want you hellishly in hell!

ISABELLE. Ah want you in the basement – even though
    we've no goat wan!

YANNICK. Ah want you oan a water-bed – even though we've
    no goat wan!

ISABELLE. Ah want you oan the balcony so's the neighbours hear us, so's the street hears us, so's the city hears us! Ah want you so's the haill world can hear us!

YANNICK. Ah want you!

ISABELLE. Ah want you!

YANNICK. Ah want you!

ISABELLE. Ah want you!

ISABELLE. Ah want you in a see-through sarong!

YANNICK. Ah want you bra-less in a thong!

ISABELLE. Ah want you in a rubber suit!

YANNICK. Ah want you in chocolate fae head tae foot!

ISABELLE. Ah want you that much it's no real!

YANNICK. Ah want you that much ah feel no weel!

ISABELLE. Will we dae it?

YANNICK. Will we dae it?

ISABELLE. Will we dae it there, oan the pavement?

YANNICK. Will we dae it there, jist tae try it?

YANNICK, ISABELLE. Will we dae it there in front ae everybody? . . . (*Silence.*) . . . Naw, but we'll dae it in thirty seconds fae now!

They run up the stairs.

YANNICK, ISABELLE. Evenin!

ROSE. Evenin . . .

They shut the door brusquely.

THE NINE OTHERS *look at the moon.*

YVON. Twenty-two, twenty-one, twenty, nineteen, eighteen . . .

GÉRARD *smiles.*

IV

DE PROFUNDIS et GLORIA

largo

THE NINE CHARACTERS (*in unison, very precisely*).
O moon, O blood of Christ. O moon, O blood of Christ,
in your passage across the sky. O moon, O blood of Christ,
in your passage across the sky, bring me peace. I cast my
gaze upon you. Hear me. Hear me. Pour your blood-red
gaze upon me and hear my prayer. My life is falling apart.
My soul is in tatters. Help me. Bring me peace. O moon,
O blood of Christ. O moon, O blood of Christ, in your
passage across the sky. O moon, O blood of Christ, in your
passage across the sky, bring me peace.

[YVON, GÉRARD. O moon, O blood of Christ . . .

MATHIEU. It's hopeless.

MIREILLE. It's hopeless.]

[ROSE, THE WIDOW. O moon, O blood of Christ, in your
passage across the sky . . .

MATHIEU. Hear me.

MIREILLE. Hear me.

MATHIEU. Cast your gaze upon me.]

[JEANNINE, LOUISE. O moon, O blood of Christ, in your
passage across the sky, bring me peace.

MIREILLE. Ma life is fallin apart.

MATHIEU. Help me.

MIREILLE. Help me.

MATHIEU. Help me.]

THE NINE CHARACTERS. Hear me.

THE WIDOW. My soul is in tatters.

GÉRARD. Help me.

GASTON. Bring me peace.

ROSE. Help me.

GÉRARD. O moon, O blood of Christ, in your passage across
the sky, bring me peace . . . just a little . . . a little peace . . .

YVON. Bring me peace.

THE WIDOW. From the depths of my misery, I lift up my
eyes . . .

MATHIEU. I lift up my eyes to you . . .

THE WIDOW, MATHIEU. And I ask you to have mercy upon
me.

THE NINE CHARACTERS. O moon, O blood of Christ, in
your passage across the sky, bring me peace. From the
depths of my misery, I lift up my eyes to you and ask you to
have mercy upon me.

MIREILLE. See, look! Aw ae a sudden it's turnt fae red tae
white.

ROSE. It's turnt white aw ae a sudden.

YVON. It's as if it's a different moon fae the red wan came out
behind the houses . . .

JEANNINE. . . . it's a white moon sailing high in the sky like a
great galleon!

THE NINE CHARACTERS. The summer moon in all its
glory! In all its glory! In all its glory!

MATHIEU. Hear me.

THE WIDOW. Hear me.

MIREILLE. Help me.

GÉRARD. Console me.

LOUISE. Console me.

GASTON. Try tae console me, even if ah am inconsolable.

THE NINE CHARACTERS. O moon, O blood of Christ.
O moon, O blood of Christ, in your passage across the sky.
O moon, O blood of Christ, in your passage across the sky,
bring me peace. Bring me a little peace. Grant me a little of
your glory. Bring a little peace to my sufferings. Bring me
peace.

JEANNINE. Higher!

LOUISE. Higher!

THE WIDOW. Hang your glory in the heights of heaven!

ROSE. But grant me jist a little.

LOUISE. Let your milk-white gaze . . .

[. . . pour over me.

JEANNINE. Your milk-white gaze . . .

. . . your healing light.

MIREILLE. Your healin light.]

THE NINE CHARACTERS. Your light. Your glory. Your
peace. O moon, let your milk-white gaze pour over me. O
host of heaven, let your light flow over me. Let your light
flow over me. Bathe me in your peace. Bathe me in your
peace. Your peace. Peace. Peace. Peace. Peace . . .

V

DIES IRAE

allegro agitato

JEANNINE, LOUISE, ROSE, MATHIEU, GASTON, GÉRARD,
THE WIDOW, *all together, very slowly throughout all of this
fast movement.*

[JEANNINE. I've no peace . . . I've no peace anymore.

LOUISE. I've no peace . . . I've no peace anymore.

MATHIEU. I've no peace . . . I've no peace anymore.

ROSE. Ah've no peace . . . Ah've no peace anymair.

GÉRARD. Ah've no peace . . . Ah've no peace anymair.

WIDOW. Ah've nae peace . . . Ah've nae peace anymair.

GASTON. Ah've nae peace . . . Ah've nae peace anymair.]

*The outer pair of the following four lines are said four
times.*

| YVON. Ah've no peace . . .

[. . . Ah've no peace anymair.

MIREILLE. Ah've nae peace . . .]

| . . . Ah've nae peace anymair.

YVON. Ah've had enough.

MIREILLE. Ah've had enough.

MIREILLE, YVON. Ah cannae cope anymair.

MIREILLE. Ah've had it up tae here wi skivvyin fur ye, dad.
   Ah've had ma fill ae daein fur ye – waashin yir face, wipin
   yir erse, seein tae yir ivry need. Ah'm sick ae no hivin a life
   tae masel, ae no hivin a life ae ma ain. Aw cos ah've tae
   look eftir you. Wance'n fur aw, ah waant a bit ae peace!

YVON. Ah cannae cope wi goin on like this, understand? Ah
cannae go on actin the nurse, comin back here fae ma work
and no knowin in what state ah'll find ye. Ah cannae go on
any longer. Ah've had enough ae it! Ah'm worn oot. Worn
oot and sick wi worry. D'ye understand? Ah spend aw ma
time at work watchin the telephone. Ma nerves are
shattered!

MIREILLE *and* YVON *repeat the same two speeches,
saying them at the same time.*

YVON. Ah've had enough!

MIREILLE. Ah've had enough!

YVON, MIREILLE. Ah've had enough ae cleanin up your
shite!

YVON. Your shite, Gérard, your shite! Ah'm sick ae cleanin up
your shite! Ah'm sick ae wipin yir arse, ae washin yir arse
while fightin back ma tears and tryin no tae spew up, sick
ae changin the sheets, disinfectin ivrythin, then startin
again, startin aw ower again wi nae prospect ae it ever
comin tae an end, wi nae hope it'll ever finish, unless . . .
(*He stops suddenly and looks at* GÉRARD.) . . . unless you
pass away . . . My God, unless you pass away!

MIREILLE. Ever since ah wis wee, ever since mum passed
away cos she couldnae take anymair ae it, ah've hid tae dae
her duties. But noo it's ma turn no tae be able tae cairry
oan. It's ma turn tae waant tae pack it aw in. Ever since ah
wis a lassie ah've served ye hand and fit – been yir cook, yir
cleaner, yir nurse, yir skivvy. But ah'm seeck-scunnered
actin the servant!

YVON. Ah didnae fall in love wi you thirty year ago so's tae
end up watchin ye spewin yir guts up intae a basin! Ah'm
no acceptin it! Ah'm tired ae watchin yir every breath, yir
every move. Ah cannae go on watchin fur the least wee new
red spot on yir body and listenin oot for the least wee shout
in the night! And ae countin yir pills! And ae handin them
tae ye! And ae cajolin ye tae take them! And ae forcin them
one bi one doon yir throat when ye refuse because they
make ye even sicker! Jesus Christ! Jesus, Jesus Christ!

Ah've had enough ae watchin you dyin slowly, seein death
in yir eyes! Ah loved your eyes but noo ah hate them – ah
see only death in them!

MIREILLE. It's because ae you ah nivir hid any friends.
They'd ayewis end up bein nosey aboot ye. They thoat ah
wis funny in the heid tae've sacrificed masel fur ma faither.
But it's no as if ah had a choice – ah'd nae choice!

YVON. Ah don't dare go oot anymair, ah don't dare phone up
anybody anymair cos ah'm sick ae wir friends' nosey
questions. Sick ae their pity . . . their friggin pity! And the
insinuations at the back ae it, cos they know how you goat
it, this disease.

MIREILLE. Ah wis always the Sister ae Mercy, the nice wan
who looks efter her crippled faither. . . .

YVON. Ah've been the Sister ae Mercy for too long, the nice
wan who looks efter his sick chum . . .

MIREILLE. Ah'm scunnered!

YVON. Ah'm scunnered!

MIREILLE. Ah waant tae smash ivrythin!

YVON. Ah want tae smash ivrythin tae smithereens! Tae burn
the haill loat! Because ah'm feart! Because ah'm feart ah'll
lose you! Because ah'm feart ah'll lose maself as well! Lose
who ah am in bitterness and spite! Ah want you tae be ill
because yir illness is proof you wur unfaithful, and ah'm
angry you're angry because you think that's terrible. Ah
look at the moon and ah tell maself it might be the last
wan you'll see, and ah'm terrified! Ah'd prefer tae destroy
ivrythin than go oan livin in uncertainty like this! Sometimes at nights, in the hour or two ye're able tae sleep, ah
feel ah could lean over ye and scream: Go! Go! Go, here'n
now, go! Cos ah cannae stand livin like this anymair!

MIREILLE. Ah cannae go oan feedin ye, faither, huddin yir
soup spoon, yir foark, wipin yir mooth when ye dribble! It
drives me demented! Fur fifteen years, dad, ah've fed ye
three times a day, and three times a day doon aw thae years
ah've felt like stranglin ye! What could you dae, dad, eh?

What could you dae wi thae piggin wee stumps if ah wis tae
try tae strangle ye! Eh? Wi thae piggin wee stumps that've
stoapped us livin like ither folk aw thae years? Ah feel like
smashin ivrythin, settin fire tae the place, poisonin the two
ae us, cuttin ma throat even, leavin you tae fend fur yirsel
wi yir bastardin work accident! Ivry moarnin ah wake up
angry, ivry single moarnin! Ah know whit the neighbours
say aboot us. Aboot how we make a couple, the pair ae us.
The durty jokes they crack behind oor backs, the questions
they ask thirsels aboot us, the lies they make up. Ah feel
like shoutin at them: Aye, it's true, ah dae aw that! Ah dae
aw that fur him, and mebbe ah dae even mair than you
think! Ma faither's a man wi a man's needs! Efter that, ah'd
be as well slittin ma wrists . . . be better aff deid. There's
jist nae end tae it! Ah kin see nae end! Nae end! Nane!
Jesus Christ! Jesus Christ!

YVON. Ah didnae deserve this!

MIREILLE. Ah didnae deserve this!

YVON (*changing his tone*). You didnae either, ah know . . .

MIREILLE. You didnae either . . . ah know . . .

YVON. You didnae deserve . . .

[. . . this disease . . .

MIREILLE. You didnae deserve . . .]

. . . that accident

YVON. Mebbe you chased efter it, but ye didnae deserve it . . .

MIREILLE. Mebbe you wis careless wance too oaffen, but you
didnae deserve it . . .

YVON (*in his original tone*). But here'n noo, the-night, at this
very minute, ah feel like showin you nae sympathy. Ah feel
like tellin you tae fuck off, tae fuck off and die!

MIREILLE. Ah know the life ye hiv, but ah'm no interested in
that the-night, ah'm only interested in ma life, the life ah
hivtae live! Let me be selfish jist for wance!

YVON. Let me be selfish jist for wance!

MIREILLE. And howl!

YVON. And howl at the moon!

MIREILLE. Even if ah'm punished efterwards . . .

YVON. Even if ah'm punished efterwards . . .

YVON, MIREILLE. . . . fur no bein carin. Ah've had enough ae carin. It's no true ah'm perfect, and kind, and selfless . . . Ah'm selfish and cruel and sick-scunnered!

YVON. And when the time fur punishment comes . . .

MIREILLE. And if wan day the time tae pey comes . . .

YVON, MIREILLE. Well Christ, ah'll pey! But right now . . . ah'm too worn doon tae go oan, too worn doon tae stoap . . .

THE SEVEN OTHERS (*very slowly and quietly*). Lord, have mercy upon us.

YVON, MIREILLE (*very quietly*). A . . . men.

VI

LUX AETERNA

andante

JEANNINE, LOUISE (*lagging by a few words,* LOUISE*'s speech echoes* JEANNINE*'s, a little similar to two people saying the same prayer*). Why does the full moon always have this effect on me? It's the light, I suppose. It puts me at peace. The eternal light of the triumphant full moon. Once a month . . . one night a month, its white light pours over me, healing my wounds. In winter I sit in the dark at the window watching it rise; in summer I go out on the balcony and let its white light pour over me. My comfort. My solace. Peace.

THE SEVEN OTHERS. Peace.

YVON. Ah've no peace . . .

[. . . ah've no peace anymair.

MIREILLE. Ah've nae peace . . .]

. . . ah've nae peace anymair.

LOUISE, JEANNINE (JEANNINE*'s speech now echoes* LOUISE*'s*). Peace. To know that, whatever else happens, there's at least one night, a whole night, an entire night, when I'm calm. A night when the moon cleaves the sky in two . . . healing . . . healing everything. Some people get anxious when it comes, some turn strange, some become restless and toss and turn in their sleep. But not me. The moon cradles me. The moon calms me. The moon makes me well again. I don't know why the full moon has this effect on me . . . I suppose it's the light that makes me feel peaceful like this. The eternal light of the triumphant full moon. Once a month. . . . one night a month, its white light pours over me, healing my wounds. My comfort. My solace. Peace.

THE SEVEN OTHERS. Peace.

YVON. Ah've no peace . . .

[. . . ah've no peace anymair.

MIREILLE. Ah've nae peace . . .]

. . . Ah've nae peace anymair.

JEANNINE, LOUISE (*at the same time*). But not tonight.

They look at each other for a few seconds.

JEANNINE. Tonight, I could bare my claws. I could tear and slash the sky apart, could rip the moon out like a cyst, gouge it out as if it were a malignant tumour!

LOUISE. Tonight, there's something else going on I don't understand . . .

JEANNINE. Tonight, there's a storm rampaging across the little peace I have.

LOUISE. Something that's not coming from me . . .

JEANNINE. Tonight, peace is impossible. Beyond my grasp. Beyond reach . . . Completely beyond reach . . .

LOUISE. Tonight, there's something coming from her that makes me scared.

JEANNINE. Tonight, there's a storm of words flattening everything in its path. . . .

LOUISE. Something I see in her eyes when she's drunk . . . but she hasn't been drinking tonight . . . she hasn't been drinking tonight . . . What I see in her eyes shouldn't be there . . .

JEANNINE. Terrifying words. Too many. Too many. My God, too many!

LOUISE. Violence!

JEANNINE. Tonight, I curse the words that don't do justice to the horror I feel. The nameless horror inside me that I can't stifle. The horror that crushes even my will to choke it.

LOUISE. That's what I see in her eyes tonight, violence.

JEANNINE. Boredom.

LOUISE. Violence.

THE SEVEN OTHERS. Peace.

JEANNINE. Disinterest.

LOUISE. Violence.

THE SEVEN OTHERS. Peace.

JEANNINE. Coldness.

LOUISE. Violence.

THE SEVEN OTHERS. Peace.

JEANNINE. Apathy.

LOUISE. Violence.

THE SEVEN OTHERS. Peace.

JEANNINE. Callousness.

LOUISE. Violence.

THE SEVEN OTHERS. Peace.

JEANNINE. Insensitivity.

LOUISE. Violence.

THE SEVEN OTHERS. Peace.

JEANNINE. Indifference.

LOUISE. Violence.

THE SEVEN OTHERS. Peace.

JEANNINE. Distrust.

LOUISE. Violence.

THE SEVEN OTHERS. Peace.

JEANNINE. Contempt.

LOUISE. Violence.

THE SEVEN OTHERS. Peace.

JEANNINE. Contempt.

LOUISE. Violence.

THE SEVEN OTHERS. Peace.

JEANNINE. Contempt.

LOUISE. Violence.

THE SEVEN OTHERS. Peace.

JEANNINE. Contempt.

LOUISE. Violence.

THE SEVEN OTHERS. Peace.

JEANNINE. For the first time in years I feel contempt for her.
I look at her and what I feel is even deeper than indifference.
I can't even say she's become like a stranger. You feel you
want to speak to a stranger, get to know them. It's the
opposite of being like a stranger. It's somebody you're
familiar with and know far too well. Understand too well.
Can read too well. It's a new feeling and it terrifies me.
Maybe it's been building up for a long time? I don't know,
but tonight it's come to the surface. I can't ignore it. I can't
deny it. Just thinking that she could touch me in bed in a
few minutes makes me shudder . . . And I'm angry! I'm
angry because I don't want to feel like this. It's ugly. It's
disturbing. It's suffocating me. Choking my soul, my head,
my mind . . .

LOUISE. Here it comes. The violence.

JEANNINE. . . . I want to hit her! I want to hit her! To punish
her for this feeling I have!

LOUISE. Here it is.

JEANNINE. To hit her like I do when I've been drinking.

LOUISE. Lord . . .

JEANNINE. My God . . .

LOUISE. . . . have mercy upon me.

JEANNINE. . . . have mercy upon me. I would never, ever, ever have believed that this could happen. Never. The love of my life. My great passion. Her I've given everything to, taught all I know . . . expecting nothing back in return . . . even though she gave me . . . everything. When I met her she had nothing and knew nothing, but because I loved her I made something of her. I made her something more than presentable, and then I showed her off. I showed her off with such love. I showed her the world with such love. And without any condescension. I'm positive of that. Without realising it, I was her Pygmalion and I thought I would love her forever. I loved her so much. I loved her so much. My God! That's in the past now though. I don't love her anymore. Indifference. Apathy. Coldness. Contempt. Contempt. I don't love her anymore. Oh God, the horror of not loving anymore! Worse even than the loss of desire is the horror of not loving anymore.

They look at each other for a few seconds.

YVON. It doesnae mean ah don't love you. On the contrary.

MIREILLE. It disnae mean ah don't love ye.

YVON, MIREILLE. But ah've had enough.

LOUISE. What's happening? Tell me what's happening.

JEANNINE. That's not true . . . I don't even feel like hitting her . . . I just have contempt for her.

They look at the moon.

JEANNINE, LOUISE. Go away! Go away! Go away!

THE SEVEN OTHERS. Lord, grant us peace . . . May the eternal light of peace descend upon us.

JEANNINE, LOUISE. Go away!

VII

LIBERA ME

andante – animando un poco

During the entire monologue by LOUISE, *the choir and* JEANNINE *will speak very quietly and in alternation.*

ROSE, MATHIEU, GASTON, GÉRARD, THE WIDOW.
Peace . . . peace . . . peace . . .

YVON. Ah've no peace . . .

[. . . ah've no peace anymair . . .

MIREILLE. Ah've nae peace . . .]

. . . Ah've nae peace anymair . . .

JEANNINE. Contempt. Indifference. Insensitivity. Apathy. Coldness. Distrust. Callousness. Etc.

LOUISE. Please, God, help me . . . to ignore my suspicion. Help me to put it out of my head. I'm sorry if that's a coward's way out, but I can't face confronting the truth. If you think I'm wrong acting this way, give me some kind of sign so's this living hell is put an end to once and for all. Because I know that the day I'm certain my suspicion is justified will be awful. I won't be able to bear it. My life will fall apart and my anger will explode . . . wild raging anger I won't be able to control! Destroy me before then, for I can't imagine life without her . . . without her body, her soul, her eyes on me, reassuring me, without her lips to kiss and the words she speaks. Life isn't worth living without her . . . Destroy her as well! She has no right to survive me! I'd refuse to go without her . . . I'd drag her into eternity with me! I'm shaking . . . shaking with anger because . . . I'm in her debt . . . everything I know, she taught me . . . but just the same, she enjoyed acting the teacher, so she did. She'd have no right to survive me! No right at all! Have mercy upon me. Take this anger away.

Take away my suspicion, my doubt. Make her indifference
and apathy towards me go away. Make her stop being
callous and cold. Most of all, let her violence be because
she's stressed, not because she feels contempt for me . . .
Oh, dear God, I've said it . . . that word! . . . Don't let her
feel contempt for me . . . I couldn't stand it. I see it in her
eyes, in her lips . . . contempt . . . contempt . . . When did
it start? When did she first start to feel that way? Was it
when we lay in bed and she looked at my body? Was it
when she was on top of me? Or when she was crouched
between my legs? Is it my fault? Has my body become
repulsive? Is it just that time changes things? Is it you being
vengeful? No, why would you? You're too great for that, too
good, too merciful. But I don't need your mercy. I haven't
done anything. I haven't done anything. I haven't done
anything to deserve this. I haven't done anything to deserve
this suspicion that's torturing me. Dear God, grant me a
little peace. Grant me a little rest. Keep that word away
from my thoughts . . . contempt. Grant me a little rest.

VIII

SANCTUS

allegretto

ISABELLE *and* YANNICK *come out of their flat.*

ISABELLE. Wait a wee while. Surely ye kin wait a wee while, eh? We'll go back in a minute . . .

YANNICK. Okay, but we'll dae it, eh? . . . Dae it aw night . . . and forever . . . till death us do part . . .

ISABELLE. Till death us whit? Come aff it! D'you really believe that?

YANNICK. Absolutely!

ISABELLE. And they say it's girls ur the romantics.

ISABELLE *looks in the direction of* JEANNINE *and* LOUISE*'s balcony.*

ISABELLE. Think they still dae it as much as us?

YANNICK. For their sakes ah hope so . . . But ah doubt it . . . we nivir hear thum . . .

ISABELLE. Think they aw hear us?

YANNICK. Ah hope so!

Silence.

[ROSE. Look, the moon his croassed the street . . .

GASTON. Look, the moon his croassed the street . . .]

ISABELLE. Look, the moon his croassed the street . . . while we wur daein it . . . it'll go in a minute . . .

MATHIEU. Let it go . . .

MIREILLE. Lea it go . . .

[MATHIEU. I don't care . . .

MIREILLE. Ah dinnae care . . .]

THE WIDOW, ROSE. Ye hiv tae lean oot tae see it noo . . .

YANNICK. Aye, but ye kin still see it fae oor bedroom . . . when we go back tae bed we'll be daein it in bright moonlight . . .

GÉRARD. It'll be too bright in the bedroom the-night . . .

YVON. We'll pull the blind . . .

GÉRARD. Fine well you know ah see the full moon even through the blind and it stops me fae gettin tae sleep . . .

YVON. You kin put on yir mask . . .

GÉRARD. Ah don't like puttin that mask on . . .

YVON *sighs.*

GÉRARD. Ah'm sorry. Ah'm gettin on yir nerves . . .

YVON. You said it.

YANNICK. It's funny tae think the moon's above the buildin, lightin up the back lane, shinin intae the flat, spotlightin the bed wi the sheets aw messed up and the smell ae us . . .

ISABELLE. Watchin over us . . .

YANNICK. Watchin over us. . . .

ISABELLE. . . . blessed moon . . .

YANNICK. . . . . blessed moon . . .

ISABELLE, YANNICK. Blessed moon, starin doon on us . . .

THE WIDOW. Dinnae shift . . .

ROSE. Blessed, holy moon . . .

ROSE, ISABELLE, YANNICK. . . . . starin doon on us . . .

THE WIDOW. Dinnae shift. Dinnae shine yir light oan my empty bed . . .

MATHIEU. I wish it would go away . . .

MIREILLE. Ah waant it tae go away . . .

ISABELLE, YANNICK, ROSE. . . . blessed moon, take care
ae us . . .

ROSE. . . . take care ae him . . . take care ae him . . . my boy . . .
take care ae my boy . . .

THE WIDOW. . . . dinnae shine yir light oan my misery . . .

ROSE. . . . take care ae my boy . . .

THE WIDOW. . . . oan my loneliness . . .

ROSE. . . . my boy . . .

THE WIDOW. . . . my sair loss . . .

LOUISE. Set me free!

JEANNINE. Let me go!

GÉRARD. Set me free!

GASTON. Let me go!

LOUISE, JEANNINE, GÉRARD, GASTON. Or leave us alone!

ISABELLE, YANNICK, THE WIDOW, ROSE. . . . Blessed,
holy moon . . . starin doon on us from high above . . .
heaven and earth are filled wi your glory . . . take care
ae us . . .

YVON. There's not a breath ae air . . . nothin is movin . . . the
moon is at its highest point . . . From now on, fae this very
second, it'll start tae set towards the west . . . The lamp of
night, starin doon on us, starts its slow journey towards
mornin.

ROSE, THE WIDOW. There's not a breath ae air . . .

ISABELLE, YANNICK. . . . nothin is movin . . .

JEANNINE, LOUISE. The moon is at its highest point . . .

GÉRARD, GASTON. From now on . . .

ROSE, THE WIDOW, YANNICK, ISABELLE, GASTON,
GÉRARD, JEANNINE, LOUISE. . . . from this very
second . . .

ALL THE CHARACTERS. . . . it starts its slow journey
towards morning . . .

YVON. The lamp of night.

THE OTHERS. The lamp of night.

ALL THE CHARACTERS. The lamp of night, staring down
on us from high above, starts its slow journey towards
morning.

YVON. Take care of me . . .

THE OTHERS. Take care of me . . .

YVON. Set me free . . .

[THE OTHERS. Set me free!

ISABELLE, YANNICK. Take care of me!]

MATHIEU. Set me free!

MIREILLE. Set me free!

MATHIEU, MIREILLE. Set me free! Let me go!

THE WIDOW. Stey!

YANNICK. Stey!

ISABELLE. Stey!

ROSE. Stey!

THE WIDOW, ROSE, YANNICK, ISABELLE. Stey nailed tae
the middle ae the sky! Crucified in the heights o' heaven!

ALL THE CHARACTERS (*except* MATHIEU *and*
MIREILLE). Blessed, holy moon.

IX

RECORDARE

adagio maestoso

ROSE. Wid ye like somethin? Cup ae tea . . .

MATHIEU. No. Nothin . . .

ROSE. Dinnae let things get ye doon. Ah don't know what tae
say or what tae dae. . . . Ah don't know what ah kin say or
dae . . .

MATHIEU. Leave it be . . . There's nothin to be done. . . .
Nothin to say . . . There's no point. . . . Leave it be, mum . . .
There's nothin to be done . . . Nothin to say . . . There's no
point . . .

MATHIEU *continues to repeat these same phrases quietly
during* ROSE*'s monologue.*

THE WIDOW (*even more quietly and more slowly than*
MATHIEU). Dinnae shift . . . Stey there . . . Dinnae leave
me masel . . . Dinnae shift . . . Stey there. . . . Dinnae leave
me masel . . . etc.

ROSE (*looking up at the sky*). Ye cannae see it noo. Ye kin jist
feel its light . . . (*Silence while the other two continue.*) Is it
the day of judgement? Is it already the day of judgement?
Dae you remember? My God, who's supposed tae come
doon here tae redeem oor sins, dae you remember ah broat
up this boy on ma own, gien him aw the love ah could, aw
the love ah could? Dae ah hivtae pey a price over and above
that? Hivtae feel guilty fur his unhappiness? Fur
unhappiness ah cannae understand? Ah greet like ah'm
guilty, ah hide ma face as if ah'd committed a big sin, ah
punish masel fur ma son's unhappiness as if ah wis tae
blame. Kin you understand that? Plus ah cannae console
him. Ah finish up jist sayin stupid things tae him cos ah
cannae understand why he's greetin because anither man
has left him! Ah thoat because ah loved him ah could

understand everythin, could accept everythin. Accept that he
leaves his wife, leaves his wee laddie, gies up his guid joab,
then turns tae men efter bein mairried, for he'd always been
that wey inclined he says . . . Ah boattled everythin up, ah
held ma tongue, ah tried tae understand, ah tried. Ah tried
bi tellin masel it wis his life tae live, that his happiness wis
his business, but aw that time ah wis jist foolin masel. Ah
would've preferred hid he steyed the Mathieu ah broat up,
leadin a quiet life, nothin special, ordinary . . . ordinary but
safe. Ah fooled masel, pattin masel oan the back fur bein
an understandin mother, able tae accept anythin because ah
loved ma son. But that wisnae true. So long as he wis happy
ah could accept how he'd turnt oot, even if ah wis secretly
hopin aw the while it wis somethin temporary, but noo that
he's sufferin and ah feel helpless, aw ma bitterness rises tae
the surface again. Ah could pour it aw oot, swearin'n cursin,
blasphemin, unless you help me. Unless you help me no tae
blaspheme you, no tae curse'n swear at you. Because it's
easier tae curse you than tae speak tae ma boy. Ah don't hiv
the words, dae you understand that? Ah don't hiv the words
tae comfort him because ah don't understand his hurt! No,
no, ah dae understand his hurt. Ah understand his sufferin
fur ah've awready suffered in the same wey. But ah don't
understand how he suffers because ae a, how a man
kin make him suffer! It's no my fault! It's no through any
ill-will! And deep doon, truth tae tell . . . my God, ah'm
weary. Ah miss him. Ah miss what he wis before. Ah hid
nae worries aboot the life he wis livin then . . . the future
held nae worries . . . and he hid his faimly . . . how ah miss
them . . . Aye, ah admit it, though ah feel guilty sayin that,
tae, fur ah know that's aw ower wi, finished and done wi!
Is that pure and simple selfish? Aw that time, wis ah bein
selfish withoot realisin it? And is that how ah'm bein
punished noo? Ah always thoat you punished in a fair
wey, but this . . . dear Jesus! At least make this weariness,
aw this hurt serve some purpose . . . Speak tae me . . .
gie me . . . gie me the words tae comfort him. Ah cannae
bear seein him like that . . . Ah'll go oan chokin back
everythin . . . bitin ma tongue. Ah'll no criticise him, ah'll
keep everythin tae masel. He'll nivir suspect anythin, ah

promise. But help me tae find the right words. Do you hear
me? Are you even listenin? Do you take the trouble tae
listen tae us or do ye jist make us believe that so's we'll
shut up? Do you laugh at me behind ma back, hidin behind
yir moon there, stretched oot oan yir cloud, listenin mair tae
yir angels' harps and yir damned saints? Eh? Dae you exist?
Dae you even exist? Dae you even hear me or am ah pourin
ma hert oot fur nothin?

The other two characters continue for a few seconds.

ROSE (*coldly*). Excuse me fur beggin you like this . . . You
mebbe hiv mair important things tae think aboot.

MATHIEU *and* THE WIDOW *speak more and more
quietly.*

X

LIBER SCRIPTUS et AGNUS DEI

allegro agitato

ALL THE CHARACTERS (*except* ROSE). You maybe have more important things to think about.

ROSE. Ah, well . . . ah kin wait ma turn. There're folk worse aff than me . . . Ah kin go oan tryin tae comfort ma son till ma time's up. Till you git roond tae me.

ALL THE CHARACTERS. Everything is written in your big book. Everything. Every single thing.

ISABELLE, YANNICK. Ah . . . it's almost dark noo . . .

THE WIDOW. Mebbe it's away forivir . . .

ROSE. Keep me in darkness . . .

MIREILLE. Ah think ah'll away tae ma bed. It's too late tae think aboot gaun oot noo . . .

THE WIDOW. Sometimes it serves nae purpose tae beg, eh?

ROSE. But when ma time comes, gie me a warnin . . . When you reach ma name, when ma time comes and you get roond tae judgin me, ah'll be ready . . .

ALL THE CHARACTERS. Nothing I say or do is forgotten, everything is written forever and ever in your big book, everything is taken into account, everything is weighed, measured, judged . . . But when my time comes, give me warning . . . Then, when you reach my name, when the time comes and you get round to judging me, I'll be ready . . .

ISABELLE, YANNICK. But don't be too hard oan us for havin loved too much, for no considerin others . . . Forgive us our selfishness . . . and try tae forget what's no nice about us . . . because we arenae always nice . . .

THE OTHERS. Don't be too hard on us . . .

ALL THE CHARACTERS. Read what isn't written. When you reach my page, when you read my life, when you're about to pronounce your judgement on my time down here, when you read my blasphemies and my trespasses, take into account my great sorrows. I know that everything has to be revealed and judged, but before tearing out my paltry page, before crumpling it up, before flinging it into terrifying eternity, consider how the sorrows you have sent are at times too much to understand, too much to bear. Please remember that I'm only a poor suffering mortal who resorts to blasphemy to ease their pain. What else can I do?

ISABELLE. Ah don't like this darkness . . .

YANNICK. Pit yir airms roon me . . .

ISABELLE. Hold me tight!

ALL THE CHARACTERS. Till that time, cast your great white gaze upon people unhappier than me . . . Maybe you have more important things to think about . . . Maybe you have more important things to see to. I . . .

GASTON. No!

GÉRARD. No!

MIREILLE. No!

LOUISE. Don't leave!

ROSE. Don't go away!

THE WIDOW. Stey!

YVON. Stey!

MATHIEU. Stay!

JEANNINE. Stay!

ISABELLE, YANNICK. Come back! Ah don't like this feelin!

ALL THE CHARACTERS. You've no right! You've no right to leave me like this! Bring it back! Bring back your great white light! Leave it hanging over us forever! It's my lifeline! I need it! I need it to survive!

YANNICK. Hold me!

ISABELLE. Hold me tight!

YANNICK. Love me!

ISABELLE. Love me!

ALL THE CHARACTERS. Love me! Love me! You that expunges the sins of the world, love me! Make the sky roll back! Make the universe roll back! Bring back your great white host! Have mercy upon me! Have mercy upon me! Grant me peace!

XI

LACRYMOSA

lento

[*Translators' note: The 'Love me' below is not addressed to God, as at the end of the previous scene, but to the characters' partners – as signalled by the conjugation of the verb in the original French.*]

YANNICK. Love me . . .

ISABELLE. Love me . . .

LOUISE. Love me . . .

YANNICK. Love me . . .

ISABELLE. Love me . . .

LOUISE. Love me . . .

They continue in the same tone during the entire scene.

THE WIDOW, MATHIEU. It's durin nights like this . . . durin nights like this, hot, close, stiflin, that we were happiest.

MATHIEU. The messed-up bed . . .

THE WIDOW. The crumpled sheets, damp wi sweat . . .

MATHIEU. The smell of our sweat . . .

[. . . hangin in the air . . .

THE WIDOW. The smell ae oor sweat . . .]

. . . hangin in the air . . .

MATHIEU, THE WIDOW. His body . . . on top of mine . . . or under mine . . . his chin lifted in pleasure . . . his neck invitin ma love-bites . . . his skin sometimes bleedin . . . his blood that I licked and swallowed . . . his blood that tasted like the salt ae sweat, the salt ae blood . . . the little bite-marks in his neck . . . the sounds of our love-makin . . . his and mine together . . . the stains on the sheets . . . his stains and my stains. . . . the room . . . the room . . . the room hot, humid, heavy . . . the sweet-sour smell of his seed . . . and the great round eye ae the full moon bathin us in its milk . . . [THE WIDOW *says 'thegther' for 'together'.*]

THE WIDOW. Ah'll nivir forget that . . .

MATHIEU. I'll never forget that . . .

THE WIDOW. Ah'll nivir get over it . . .

MATHIEU. I'll never get over it . . .

THE WIDOW. No.

MATHIEU. No.

THE WIDOW. No.

MATHIEU. No.

THE WIDOW, MATHIEU. Never.

THE WIDOW. Oh, dear God . . . Ah thoat ah'd nae mair tears left. . . . But here they come . . . here they come . . . It's been that long . . . Oh, aye, let me greet . . . let me greet . . . Oh, aye, let me greet . . . For ma lost happiness . . . lost forivir . . .

MATHIEU. Let me cry. Please. Let me cry. You seem to be stoppin me. I can't find the tears. I can't find them! If I could just breathe in this humid night air and fill myself with tears again. Please. I haven't cried enough . . . and I'm tired . . . I'm down . . . exhausted. You bring me to the edge of tears, tease me, and then you turn your back on me. You leave me lookin intae emptiness . . . feelin sick . . . and wantin tae die.

THE WIDOW. Let me greet for the pleasure his body gien me, and mine gave his . . . for his exhaustion when we'd finished makin love and he wid say . . . Oh God, his hert wis aboot tae explode but it wis worth it . . . because . . . my God . . . because he loved me. Loved me! Let me greet for the love that held us thegither through thick and thin, for his hands, for his legs intwined wi mines, for his skin ah loved

tae kiss, for the fright ah gied him when ah moaned too
loud . . .

MATHIEU. I can't take it in that he's gone . . . gone . . . I
cannae accept it . . .

THE WIDOW. For the surprised look on his face when ah
waanted tae dae it again, though he wis pleased when we
did! Oh, how we laughed and laughed! Ah wish ah could
laugh like that again.

MATHIEU. The laughs him'n me had! He was always tellin
me he would never leave me cos nobody else made him
laugh like I did.

[THE WIDOW. How kin ah ivir get over losin aw that?

MATHIEU. How can I ever get over losin all that?]

MATHIEU. The ticklin sessions . . . the foolin about . . . the
nights spent laughin and cryin and kissin! Somethin would
jist come over me and I would cry wi thanks. . . .
Remember? . . . Somethin would come over me and I'd be
cryin and kissin and thankin you . . .

THE WIDOW. Somethin wid come ower me and ah'd be
greetin and kissin and thankin you . . . and laughin! You'd
gien me somebody sae full ae life, sae handsome and lovin.

MATHIEU. I wanted to thank you then, God . . . for havin
made me see . . . havin made me understand . . . havin made
me accept. But now I don't have the words anymore . . .
I don't even have the tears . . . I'm jist empty. Tonight, here
and now, I'd like to be attracted to nothin. Understand?
Nothin. Not women, not men, nothin! I'd like tae forget that
love even exists. That other people exist. I'd like tae find a
place tae hide in for the rest of my life. But I cannae do that.
I cannae forget. I cannae forgive. I'm empty. Jist empty.

THE WIDOW. But ah still don't understand why . . . ah still
don't accept . . . that my bed is empty!

MATHIEU. Empty!

THE WIDOW. Empty!

[THE WIDOW. It's ma first full moon since he went. Ah'm no sure ah kin get through it withoot him. My God, ah don't think ah'll ivir be able tae forgive him for leavin me.

MATHIEU. It's ma first full moon since he went. I'm not sure I can get through it without him. My God, I don't think I'll ever be able tae forgive him for leavin me.]

MATHIEU. 'I'm sorry, I can't help maself, I'm head over heels' . . . that's what he said when he left . . .

THE WIDOW. 'Ah'm sorry for leavin you all alone, ah feel like ah'm desertin you' . . . that's what he said when he left . . .

MATHIEU. I wish he was dead!

THE WIDOW. Sometimes . . . sometimes ah think he wis right . . . he did desert me . . .

MATHIEU. I wish he was dead! I'd rather he was dead than in somebody else's arms!

THE WIDOW. Ah'd raither he wis in somedy else's airms than accept ah'll nivir see him again!

MATHIEU. I wish he was dead! Dead! Dead!

THE WIDOW. Take care ae him aw the same, God. Dinnae judge him too hard. He wis a good man . . .

MATHIEU. I wish he was dead!

THE WIDOW. Oh! . . . it's as if . . .

MATHIEU. Oh!

THE WIDOW. Ah kin sense his presence . . .

MATHIEU. I can smell his sweat . . .

THE WIDOW. Mebbe it's only me . . .

MATHIEU. Mebbe it's only me . . .

THE WIDOW, MATHIEU. It's like we'd become one . . .

MATHIEU. I'll never forget. . . .

THE WIDOW. . . . the smell ae his body . . . Ah'll nivir
forget . . .

MATHIEU. . . . the smell of his body . . .

THE WIDOW. Nivir.

MATHIEU. Never.

THE WIDOW. Nivir.

MATHIEU. Never.

YANNICK. Love me . . .

ISABELLE. Love me . . .

LOUISE. Love me . . .

THE WIDOW. Nivir.

MATHIEU. Never.

THE WIDOW. Not ivir . . . not ivir . . .

XII

CONFUTATIS MALEDICTIS

largo

THE WIDOW. Nivir, nivir, nivir, nivir, nivir, nivir, nivir, nivir, nivir . . .

THE WIDOW *punctuates the entire scene with her 'nivir', very regularly, like a heart beating.*

GÉRARD. It was on a night like this . . .

YVON. Don't talk aboot that the-night . . . Ah don't want tae hear aboot it . . .

GÉRARD. Oh no? . . . There was a time when you'd ask me tae tell ye ivry detail . . .

GASTON. It's on nights like this it's worst . . .

MIREILLE. Don't start . . .

GASTON. Dinnae worry, ah'll no be askin ye tae feel sorry fur me . . .

GÉRARD. It wasn't a full moon that night, but the light and the heat were jist like this . . .

YVON, MIREILLE. Don't . . .

GÉRARD, GASTON. Listen, it'll make both ae us feel better . . .

GÉRARD. It wis a stiflin night and ah wis goin demented with nothin tae do . . . you know how ah get when it's swelterin . . .

GASTON. You dinnae understand what nights like this dae tae me. . . .

YVON, MIREILLE (*quietly*). Don't . . .

GASTON. Yir mum ayewis said if we lived in a hot country, ah'd pit her in her grave . . . Christ . . .

GÉRARD. Christ . . . if you werenae on a trip . . . you were . . . ah don't know . . . 'away on business', as you always put it . . . You were away on business and ah wis tossin and turnin in bed, feelin lonely . . .

YVON. One has a wank on such occasions, and that's that!

GÉRARD. That wasnae the problem! . . . Ah wanted company . . .

YVON. Oh aye, blame it on me . . .

GÉRARD. Ah'm no blamin you . . .

YVON. Yes, you are blamin me . . . you've blamed me since it happened . . .

GÉRARD. No ah havenae.

YVON. Yes you have! You want me tae take the blame so's ah'll think if ah'd been here that week nothin would've happened. That's what you want me tae think. Ah know fine well that's what you want me tae think. You feel guilty and ye want tae get shot ae it bi passin the blame on tae me.

GASTON. Kin you imagine how it feels when it's swelterin like the-night? Kin you imagine how it feels when the sweat's pourin aff yir face, runnin doon yir nose ticklin ye, and ye cannae even lift a haund tae wipe it?

MIREILLE. Ah know aw that. . . . ah know it . . . ma life's been full ae it fur fifteen years . . . Ah've been your hands in aw that time, dad . . . Aw that sweat, in aw that time, it's me that's sponged it aff!

YVON, MIREILLE. You always harp oan aboot the same thing!

GASTON, GÉRARD. If ah harp oan, it's because ah've been unlucky!

YVON, MIREILLE. Unlucky?!

MIREILLE. You worked for years oan a dangerous machine when ye'd been drinkin and it endit up tearin baith yir airms aff!

YVON. You took advantage ae me bein away tae go and have yirself fucked by the first man ye met!

GÉRARD. Tae tell the truth, he wasnae the first ah met . . . far from it . . .

YVON. But he'd be the first that wis young and good-lookin, though, eh?!

GÉRARD. So ah suppose it woulda been okay-dokay had ah caught it fae a fat ugly wan, is that it?

The four characters remain silent for a few seconds. THE WIDOW *continues her 'nivir, nivir, nivir, . . . '.*

GASTON. Naebdy ivir deserved somethin like this. Naebdy.

MIREILLE. No . . .

MIREILLE, YVON. Ah'm sorry . . .

GÉRARD. Ah refuse tae take any blame. D'ye hear me? Ah refuse tae feel guilty. We grew up feelin guilty fur everythin and ah've had enough ae it. Ah refuse tae feel guilty and ah refuse tae be punished!

YVON. So why then are ye wantin tae tell me how it happened?

GÉRARD. Because you assume ah regret it . . .

YVON. Meanin ye don't regret it?

GÉRARD. Ah don't know . . .

YVON. Ye don't regret it!

GÉRARD. Listen . . . listen without interruptin me. Mebbe you'll understand . . . mebbe you'll come tae understand . . .

YVON. Understand! Understand!

GÉRARD. Ah hadnae been unfaithful to ye for years. We'd passed the stage ae hurtin each other. We'd long since settled intae a rut that wis startin tae get me down . . . Ah wis actually beginnin tae feel old fur the first time in ma life. Ah wis noticin more and more that ma body wasnae what it used tae be. Even that trick mirror we'd bought couldnae hide it. When you start tae put on weight, even a trick mirror shows it! Ah didnae even feel like sex anymair . . . ah'd lost the urge . . . felt past it. Ah took the chance while you were away ae provin tae maself for one last time that . . . Ah wis sure you'd never find out about it, and ah convinced maself that you wir mebbe doin the same thing in Quebec, or Toronto, or Vancouver, or wherever the hell you were . . . Ah told maself, what he doesn't know, doesn't hurt him . . . If it's gonnae do me good, just go for it . . . just one last time. Ah swear it. Just one last time. It was a beautiful night . . . hot . . . and ah wis feelin . . . horny . . . ye know? Hornier than ah'd felt in years. Ah felt ah wanted a change . . . a skin younger than mines, younger than yours . . . the smooth, hard, young body of a stranger that wid provide me wi fantasies for the rest ae ma life in case ah never got lucky again . . . For one last time ah wanted tae take a risk, tae step ootside the safe world we'd built for wirselves . . . Nothin might've happened, ah might've met nobody, or ah might've picked up a rent-boy, had a fuck, and that was that, but somethin did happen . . . When ah found masel oan ma back in the grass, it itchin me like when ah wis young, a gorgeous face lookin doon at me, a stranger's face smilin doon at me – smilin at me, cos the guy knew he wis doin me a favour by fuckin me, ah'm convinced he never knew he wis plantin the virus in me, he jist knew he wis gien me the gift ae his beauty for a few minutes . . . When ah seen his gorgeous face between the Plough and the North Star . . . the crescent moon hangin there like an earring . . . ah felt ah could stey there for the rest ae ma life, crucified in the grass, ma two feet nailed tae the sky . . . that ah would stey there for all eternity . . . for all eternity! And then, because ah knew it would be. . . . inelegant, to be caught in that position . . . ah burst out laughin! A belly laugh! A belly laugh ae freedom! Ah felt fabulous! If ah close ma eyes, ah can hear maself laughin! Ah see him again, wi his big gorgeous smile, and ah cannae hate him. Despite what's happened since that night, despite the hell ah've been through . . . the crutches, the pills, the fuckin incontinence, ah regret nothin! Ah feel guilty aboot nothin! It wis good! Can you understand that?

YVON. No. Ah'm goin tae take care ae ye, ah'm goin tae look efter ye till the very end, and ah'll be broken-hearted come the time, but don't ask me tae understand . . .

GÉRARD. Never?

YVON. Never.

GÉRARD. Awright. Ah'll never speak about it again. Never.

GASTON. When it's braw like this . . . hoat'n humid . . . ye know what it does tae me, don't ye? It only happens in the summer-time . . . in the winter ah'm like dry wid, fit fur nothin . . . But when it's swelterin like the-night . . . ah've goat ma airms back! Ah don't know how tae explain that tae ye . . . Ah dinnae sleep, so it cannae be a dream . . . and it's mair than a sensation. The feelin has nivir left me ae hivin arms and hands, ae touchin things wi ma fingers. But noo it's mair than a sensation . . . Ah swear ah could pick up a chair, ah could scratch the souls ae ma feet, the back ae ma heid . . . ah could clap even . . . D'ye understand? . . . Ah could clap ma hands like at the baseball! Ah could clap them till they wur bleedin! Ah could take ye in ma airms and fling ye intae the air! Catch ye as we fell backwards . . . and lyin there wi you in ma airms, ah'd look up at the stars, fix ma eyes oan the Plough and the North Star, and ah'd haud ye tight for aw eternity! . . . (*Silence. He howls.*) . . . Huddin somebody in ma airms. . . . How bad ah miss that. How bad ah miss it. Pittin ma airms roond somebody ah love and huddin them. . . . Huddin somebody in ma airms. Christ, tae be helpless like this! Helpless!

MIREILLE. If you hidnae been drunk that time . . .

GASTON. Ah refuse tae accept that wis God punishin me! Ah refuse tae accept it!

THE WIDOW *continues to say 'nivir' for a few seconds.*

GASTON. Oh! It's turnt pitch-black! The mass is finished!

THE WIDOW. Nivir, nivir, nivir, nivir, nivir, nivir, nivir, nivir, nivir . . .

XIII

OFFERTORY

allegro agitato

A tango played on an organ energetically, very rhythmically, and majestically, explodes suddenly. GÉRARD takes YVON's hand. The two of them go down the three steps from their balcony and begin to dance the tango on the pavement. They are rejuvenated and transformed by the music, and have the bearing and movement of young men happy and in good health. They dance very well, like a couple used to each other for many years. They smile.

The other characters, smiling also, look at them. They could even accompany them with a few 'They're good, eh?', 'Smashin dancers!', 'They make a fine couple!', 'Gaun yirsels!', etc.

One feels with GÉRARD and YVON the pure pleasure of dancing together and the awareness of how much good it is doing them.

The transubstantiation takes place. It is the offertory.

The music having ended, YVON takes refuge in GÉRARD's arms and sobs.

YVON. Don't go! Don't go! Don't go!

GÉRARD *puts his arms around him and leads him back to their place.*

XIV

ITE MISSA EST

largo

THE MEN (*quietly*). The night is pitch-black.

THE WOMEN (*quietly*). The mass is finished.

ROSE. Ah'm goantae try tae sleep oan the balcony . . .

MATHIEU. I think I'll go out . . . I don't know where . . . jist for a walk . . .

THE WIDOW. Ah'm goin tae sit here and rock masel till the sun rises.

YANNICK. Will we bring the mattress ootside?

ISABELLE. Ah'm too tired . . . ah jist want tae sleep . . .

YVON. You're late in takin yir pills . . .

GÉRARD. Aye, ah know . . . ah'm goin in tae take them . . .

YVON. Ah'm goin in as well . . .

MIREILLE. Ah'll leave the door aff the snib . . . you kin jist push it . . .

GASTON. Ah'll mebbe stey oot here till the moarnin. . . .

LOUISE. It's strange. It's so dark here, yet the moon's still shining at the back. It'll probably keep us awake . . .

JEANNINE. Moon or no moon, I wouldn't sleep . . .

A few seconds of silence.

YANNICK (*quietly*). Will we dae it again?

ISABELLE (*quietly*). You're wild . . .

YANNICK. Will we dae it again?

ISABELLE. You're wild . . .

YANNICK (*quietly*). Will we dae it again?

ISABELLE (*quietly*). You're wild . . .

They continue during the final chorus.

THE OTHERS (*quietly*). Accept this offering that I have made
from the well-spring of my soul . . . For I have poured my
soul into the immensity of the sky . . . My soul spills over
heaven . . . My soul spills over you . . . You have heard
my prayer . . . Now heaven has flooded into me . . . The
transubstantiation is complete . . . Peace . . . a little peace . . .
some comfort at last . . . has descended upon me . . . Dear
Lord . . . a little comfort . . . has poured . . . over me . . . a
little peace . . . you have granted me a little peace . . . Dear
Christ . . . have mercy upon me . . . accept my torment . . .
transform it . . . utterly . . . into peace . . . peace . . . peace . . .

JEANNINE. Amen.

LOUISE. Amen.

ROSE. Amen.

MATHIEU. Amen.

GASTON. Amen.

MIREILLE. Amen.

YVON. Amen.

GÉRARD. Amen.

THE WIDOW. Amen . . . aye . . . amen.

YANNICK. Will we dae it again?

ISABELLE. You're wild . . .

YANNICK. Will we dae it again?

ISABELLE. You're wild . . .

YANNICK. Will we dae it again?

ISABELLE. Aye!

ALL THE CHARACTERS (*very slowly, if possible sung*)
A . . . men . . .

End.